FACTOR INVESTING AND ASSET ALLOCATION

A Business Cycle Perspective

Vasant Naik, Mukundan Devarajan, Andrew Nowobilski, Sébastien Page, CFA, and Niels Pedersen

**CFA Institute
Research
Foundation**

Statement of Purpose

The CFA Institute Research Foundation is a not-for-profit organization established to promote the development and dissemination of relevant research for investment practitioners worldwide.

Cover Image Photo Credit: adventtr/Getty Images

ISBN 978-1-944960-14-8

December 2016

Editorial Staff

Ashley Bell
Product Quality Review Specialist

Julia MacKesson, PMP
Manager, Publishing, Standards and Advocacy

Anh Pham
Publishing Technology Specialist

Biographies

Vasant Naik is global head of asset allocation and empirical research in the Analytics and Quantitative Research Group at PIMCO. His team develops quantitative models to complement the macro-based analysis at PIMCO and provides asset allocation and portfolio construction advice to PIMCO's investment committees and portfolio managers. The group also develops systematic valuation models for various risk factors and asset classes. Previously, Dr. Naik was a managing director at Nomura International, where he led a team of quantitative strategists to research and advise clients on systematic investing in fixed-income markets. He has also worked at Lehman Brothers. Before joining the financial industry, Dr. Naik taught finance as a tenured faculty member at the University of British Columbia, Vancouver. His academic work is published in the *Journal of Finance, Review of Financial Studies*, and the *Journal of Financial and Quantitative Analysis*. Dr. Naik holds a PhD in finance from the University of California, Berkeley, and a postgraduate diploma in management from the Indian Institute of Management, Bangalore.

Mukundan Devarajan is an executive vice president and quantitative research analyst at PIMCO. His research focuses on building valuation models for global financial markets, identifying the determinants and predictors of asset returns, and building frameworks for top-down asset allocation. Previously, Mr. Devarajan was an executive director in the Quantitative Strategies Group at Nomura International and a director of quantitative strategies at Lehman Brothers. In these roles, he developed systematic frameworks for macro investing and advised investment institutions on asset allocation and quantitative credit selection. Mr. Devarajan has ranked highly in *Institutional Investor* surveys of fixed-income research analysts in the quantitative analysis category. He graduated from the Indian Institute of Management, Ahmedabad, where he was awarded the gold medal for scholastic performance.

Andrew Nowobilski is a senior vice president and quantitative research analyst at PIMCO, where he conducts quantitative research to advise PIMCO's portfolio managers on such issues as optimal portfolio construction for fixed-income and multi-asset portfolios, the development of valuation frameworks for macro risk factors, and analysis of portfolio risk. Dr. Nowobilski holds a bachelor's degree in economics from Duke University and a PhD in economics from Northwestern University, where he researched the macroeconomic propagation of shocks to the financial sector and channels for unconventional monetary policy.

Sébastien Page, CFA, is co-Head of the Asset Allocation Group at T. Rowe Price, overseeing a team of investment professionals dedicated to a broad set of multi-asset portfolios spanning over $230 billion in assets. Previously, and while collaborating on this book, Mr. Page was an executive vice president at PIMCO, where he led a team focused on research and development of multi-asset client solutions. Prior to joining PIMCO in 2010, he was a senior managing director at State Street Global Markets. Mr. Page won research paper awards from the *Journal of Portfolio Management* in 2003, 2010, and 2011, and from the *Financial Analysts Journal* in 2010 and 2014. He is a member of the editorial board of the *Financial Analysts Journal*. He has 18 years of investment experience and holds a master's degree in finance and a bachelor's degree in business administration from Sherbrooke University in Quebec, Canada.

Niels Pedersen is a senior vice president and quantitative research analyst at PIMCO, where he focuses on the development of quantitative investment strategies and valuation models across global asset markets. Dr. Pedersen also leads the development of the analytical framework for PIMCO's retirement target date portfolios. He has published numerous research papers on asset allocation in such publications as the *Journal of International Money and Finance*, the *Financial Analysts Journal* (2014 Graham and Dodd scroll award winner), and the *Journal of Derivatives and Hedge Funds*. Dr. Pedersen holds a bachelor's degree in economics from Aarhus University and a PhD in economics from Northwestern University, where he specialized in macroeconomics and international trade.

Contents

CE Qualified Activity ☀ CFA Institute This publication qualifies for 5 CE credits under the guidelines of the CFA Institute Continuing Education Program.

Foreword

Factor investing—building portfolios with exposure to macroeconomic or statistical factors that explain the return differences between securities—is as old as the hills. (In investing, anything older than 30 years is ancient.) Yet factor investing has only recently become a widespread practice. What is behind this sudden change in the investment management industry? What do analysts at firms that engage in factor investing do? What results might investors using these techniques expect?

About a half century ago, William Sharpe suggested that the market factor—exposure to the returns of the capitalization-weighted market portfolio—was the only factor in the equity market that was "priced" (rewarded with a higher expected return for taking the risk of being exposed to that factor). This idea is the capital asset pricing model, or CAPM.

But it quickly became evident that the CAPM did not fully explain the cross section of stock returns. Barr Rosenberg (1974) was probably the first to document the fact that stocks are correlated to factors other than the market factor. He called this phenomenon "extra-market covariance," proof of the time-honored principle that originators of great ideas should not be allowed to name them.

Rosenberg's work set off a race among researchers to find exceptions to the CAPM, called "anomalies" in their language. One of the best-known anomalies is the size effect. Rolf Banz (1981) and Marc Reinganum (1981) discovered the fact that, over time, the stocks of small firms had systematically and decisively outperformed large ones. The value effect—the tendency of cheap stocks, those with a low price-to-earnings or price-to-book-value ratio, to outperform expensive ones over significant stretches of history—was established by Sanjoy Basu (1977).

Fama and French (1992, 1993) integrated the size, value, and market factors into a single model, marking the beginning of the mass migration of assets into factor-based portfolios—although several very successful factor-based funds and strategies had been created before that. Other factors, including momentum in the equity market and various fixed-income effects, have been discovered in the years since these first efforts.

Stephen Ross, in 1976, said that stock market factors can be constructed so that they represent macroeconomic influences. His arbitrage pricing theory, developed with Richard Roll, uses factors such as GDP growth, inflation, and exchange rates to explain differences in security returns. This significant step makes it practical to use macroeconomic forecasts for alpha generation in the stock market and in other asset classes as well. The authors of this monograph likewise use "macro" information to build portfolios and adjust them over time, putting Ross's insights to practical use.

Factors are also important in fixed income and other non-equity asset classes. The classic work on fixed-income factors was done in the 1980s by Martin Leibowitz, with many co-authors,[1] although the basic concepts go back a half century further to Macaulay's (1938) discovery of duration. Credit markets involve curve and quality factors in addition to market factors such as duration and convexity. Using this kind of thinking, one can construct a top-down model of global markets that reflects the interaction of macro variables with asset-specific risk factors.

We all know that past performance is no guarantee of future results, hence the tense of the discussion: "did outperform," not "do outperform" or, heaven forbid, "will outperform."[2] Yet, if past performance provides no indication at all of how to invest for the future, there is very little else for researchers to study and we are more or less boxed into holding only index funds and abandoning the search for alpha—a bad idea whose time has not come.

Thus, analysis of past performance is crucial to the search for alpha. Marrying that quest with the macro approach and thereby building a forward-looking framework is what this research monograph is about. Specifically, it is about how "quants"—the quantitative analysts who provide the research needed to engage in factor investing—think and work. By providing richly detailed examples of the way that quants apply their techniques and thought patterns to identifying alpha opportunities across a variety of asset classes, the team of Vasant Naik, Mukundan Devarajan, Andrew Nowobilski, Sébastien Page, and Niels Pedersen show the reader what is "under the hood" at quantitative investment shops.

The authors' specific emphasis is on translating macroeconomic forecasts into alpha-generating portfolios or positions, in the spirit of arbitrage pricing theory. They focus on forming optimal portfolios of multiple asset classes. Most of the literature on factors deals with single asset classes, such as equities. But the ultimate problem of the asset owner is to allocate among asset classes. The monograph analyzes this problem via the risk factor approach. Moreover, the habits of mind revealed in this monograph are useful for understanding, developing, and implementing any kind of quantitative or factor-based approach to investing, not just one that relies on macroeconomic forecasts.

---

[1]See Fabozzi (1991).

[2]I am indebted to Cliff Asness for this comment on the tense of the language used to discuss investment performance. See Asness (2014, pp. 23–24).

We are pleased to present this extraordinary effort by a group of colleagues at one of the leading quantitative investment management firms. Readers interested in learning more about "quant" research and investing will find *Factor Investing and Asset Allocation: A Business Cycle Perspective* to be a real treat.

Laurence B. Siegel
Gary P. Brinson Director of Research
CFA Institute Research Foundation

References

Asness, Clifford S. 2014. "My Top 10 Peeves." *Financial Analysts Journal*, vol. 70, no. 1 (January/February): 22–30.

Banz, Rolf W. 1981. "The Relationship between Return and Market Value of Common Stock." *Journal of Financial Economics*, vol. 9, no. 1 (March): 3–18.

Basu, Sanjoy. 1977. "Investment Performance of Common Stocks in Relation to Their Price-Earnings Ratios: A Test of the Efficient Market Hypothesis." *Journal of Finance*, vol. 32, no. 3 (June): 663–682.

Fabozzi, Frank J. ed. 1991. *Investing: The Collected Works of Martin L. Leibowitz*. New York, McGraw-Hill.

Fama, Eugene F., and Kenneth R. French. 1992. "The Cross-Section of Expected Stock Returns." *Journal of Finance*, vol. 47, no. 2 (June): 427–465.

Fama, Eugene F., and Kenneth R. French. 1993. "Common Risk Factors in the Returns on Stocks and Bonds." *Journal of Financial Economics*, vol. 33, no. 1 (February): 3–56.

Macaulay, Frederick R. 1938. *Some Theoretical Problems Suggested by the Movements of Interest Rates, Bond Yields and Stock Prices in the United States since 1856*. New York: National Bureau of Economic Research.

Reinganum, Marc R. 1981. "Misspecification of Capital Asset Pricing: Empirical Anomalies Based on Earnings' Yields and Market Values." *Journal of Financial Economics*, vol. 9, no. 1 (March): 19–46.

Rosenberg, Barr. 1974. "Extra-Market Components of Covariance in Security Returns." *Journal of Financial and Quantitative Analysis*, vol. 9, no. 2 (March): 263–274.

Ross, Stephen A. 1976. "The Arbitrage Theory of Capital Asset Pricing." *Journal of Economic Theory*, vol. 13, no. 3: 341–360.

Preface

We are delighted that the CFA Institute Research Foundation has selected the Quantitative Research team of Pacific Investment Management Company, LLC (PIMCO), to author this monograph on quantitative approaches to asset allocation. It helps to be "macro aware" while constructing optimal portfolios—a theme the authors develop in conjunction with their emphasis on the business cycle. How does such a macro-focused approach differ from traditional approaches, in which it is customary to estimate risks and correlations only from historical asset returns?

Vasant Naik and his co-authors complement mean–variance-based portfolio optimization by emphasizing the primacy of the business cycle in determining both the risk and expected returns of risk factors. All postwar recessions in the United States have been accompanied by an increase in risk premia and elevated asset volatility. The only reliable exception to this relationship has been the risk premium for duration—that is, the term premium. More importantly, correlations among risky assets also increase during economic downturns.

The authors make these points in an elegant and simple manner by documenting the business cycle sensitivity of the average returns of major risk factors. The positive performance of bonds during recessions highlights one of the key benefits of fixed-income securities in the context of the overall portfolio.

The monograph also raises several issues related to the robustness of the historical experience, as well as the limitations of standard mean–variance optimization. For instance, the current level of global government bond yields should raise questions about both the prospective returns of government bonds and their effectiveness in hedging portfolios during future "risk off" episodes. Similarly, the negative skew observed in corporate bond spread returns highlights the need to focus on the tail risk of portfolios in addition to tracking error.

The concepts discussed in this monograph are valuable in guiding investment decisions. Should they be applied literally, especially in light of the caveats we just raised? The framework discussed in this monograph can be used to check the sensitivity of the optimal portfolio to various assumptions. Advances in technology have made it possible for practitioners to apply these portfolio analytics in real time while managing a large number of global multiasset portfolios. Investors no longer have to resort to heuristics to capture the complexity of realistic portfolio choices.

Therefore, in our view, even a mature investment process can benefit from applying scientific rigor to the various trade-offs faced by active portfolio managers. However, portfolio implementation cannot be divorced from the process of identifying alpha opportunities. While the literature on portfolio optimization is vast, there is no recipe book on how to apply these concepts in a way that complements the unique investment process and DNA of an organization.

At PIMCO, we rely on a multistage investment process. We start with a top-down consideration of the global macroeconomy. We have a structural overweight to factors with attractive risk premia. This macro-oriented process is complemented by a bottom-up analysis of value conducted by a deep bench of specialist portfolio managers. Since we expect security selection to generate a large proportion of the alpha in our portfolios, we allocate an appropriate amount of our risk budget (and resources) to this part of the process. These elements are integrated through discussions at our investment forums and investment committee meetings. All of our investment professionals meet for an entire week three times a year to discuss both the macro environment and the valuation of major risk factors. In addition, the Investment Committee meets frequently to refine and update these macro forecasts with higher-frequency data, as well as to get the perspective of the specialists.

The approach taken by the monograph reflects these features of our investment process in several important ways. The authors emphasize the use of a valuation-driven approach for estimating expected returns on asset classes. This approach blends an evolving assessment of the prospects for global growth and inflation with the valuation of risk factors. While it is convenient to think of risk in the factor space, it is important to recognize that opportunities for alpha generation present themselves in asset classes and securities. A good illustration of this distinction is the separate treatment in the monograph of the valuation of corporate credit and that of equities, even though both asset classes have a first-order exposure to the equity market factor. Marrying these two concepts—recognizing asset-specific valuation characteristics and mapping them back onto the factor space for risk management—is the key to applying many of the concepts of this monograph successfully in an investment organization.

We hope the monograph helps both the aspiring investment professional and the experienced asset manager think through the issues of portfolio construction.

Dan Ivascyn
Managing Director
Group Chief Investment Officer, PIMCO

Mihir Worah
Managing Director
Chief Investment Officer Real Return and Asset Allocation, PIMCO

Ravi Mattu
Managing Director
Global Head, Analytics, PIMCO

Acknowledgments

We are grateful to Ronald Espinosa, Tapio Pekkala, and especially Hashim Zaman for their contributions to this monograph. We also thank Jamil Baz, Helen Guo, Ravi Mattu, Rama Nambimadom, CFA, and Lutz Schloegl for their comments and suggestions.

1. Introduction

This monograph analyzes the main themes arising in top-down construction of the optimal portfolio of a global investor. Any investment process comprises a top-down component and a bottom-up component. The "top-down" part focuses on the macro risk environment and its impact on key risk factors that drive most asset returns and determines the optimal portfolio exposure to these risk factors. The bottom-up (or security selection) component, on the other hand, assesses the relative value of individual securities and firms. A good investment process should excel along both these dimensions. Our focus in this monograph is on the top-down process.

The final result of the top-down process is a set of exposures to key risk factors that represents the best trade-off between risk taken and risk premia expected to be earned. To arrive at this result, we need to answer several questions, such as how to define the key risk factors driving returns in global financial markets; how to measure and estimate risk and risk premia; how to use these estimates to construct an optimal portfolio of risk exposures; and most importantly, what we can learn about these issues from historical evidence. These are the questions that we address. Our central tenet is that risk and return in financial markets are strongly influenced by global macroeconomic fundamentals that determine the expected path of real growth, inflation, and monetary and fiscal policy, and the variability around these expectations. Therefore, we attempt to understand the macroeconomic inputs needed for optimal portfolio construction and to describe a process of portfolio formation that rests on robust macroeconomic foundations.

Another dimension that we emphasize in our discussion is the importance of market valuations in investment decision making. Understanding areas where price fluctuations have created investment opportunities is an important focus of a value-driven investment process. In this monograph, we discuss how valuations are useful, albeit imprecise, signals of risk premia. We explore approaches to tackling the difficult task of separating changes in risk premia from changes in expectations, either of which could create apparent value opportunities. While the former creates a genuine investment opportunity and the need to consider rebalancing one's portfolio, the latter does not.

The investment universe available to a global investor is vast. The first task in optimal portfolio construction is to reduce the number of decision variables in this problem. In Chapter 2, we show that there is a manageable number of risk factors that describe the core of the global investable universe. For government bonds, three or four factors describe most of the fluctuations in the entire yield curve. These factors are the short-term riskless interest rate and factors representing the shape of the yield curve at short, intermediate, and long maturities. The risk factor decomposition of bonds subject to default risk—hereafter, "default-risky bonds"—separates interest rate risk from credit risk. The yield spreads of a wide spectrum of credit market categories (in excess of government bonds) can be characterized by an overall market factor, a slope factor, and a sector factor (financials versus nonfinancials). Finally, a factor decomposition using a market index and regional and global sector factors provides a high-level representation of global equity markets.

To solve the portfolio construction problem, we need, as inputs, estimates of the volatility of various risk factors, of the correlations between them, and of the risk premia associated with them. In Chapter 3, we describe the empirical properties of these volatilities and correlations and their macroeconomic drivers. We begin with the familiar "Shiller critique" that asset markets are more volatile than fundamentals. This effect may give rise to value opportunities where prices have deviated from fundamentals. We also note that volatility and correlations tend to be countercyclical, becoming extreme in times of economic contractions and crises. This phenomenon also causes a level-dependence in the volatility of fixed-income markets, especially of credit spreads. It is important to account for all these features in portfolio risk management over a tactical horizon as well as over a longer horizon, such as the business cycle.

The second key input into optimal asset allocation is the risk premium per unit of risk (that is, the Sharpe ratio) for various risk factors. In Chapter 4, we present long-sample estimates of risk premia for key risk factors. We also discuss the dependence of realized interest rate, credit, and equity risk premia on the business cycle. While credit and equity returns have been procyclical, as expected, excess returns on interest rate duration (that is, the excess returns of long-term bonds over the short-term interest rate) have been strongly countercyclical; that is, riskless bonds outperform substantially during recessions. In addition, the stage of the business cycle matters. Equities, government bonds, and default-risky bonds outperform in early expansions. However, as expansions mature, monetary conditions tighten and slowing earnings growth increases the incidence of bondholder-unfriendly corporate actions. As a result, the performance of government bonds and credit assets suffers markedly.

A positive estimate of the risk premium for procyclical assets, such as equities and corporate bonds, is consistent with economic theory, which states that assets that underperform when investors' aggregate wealth suffers a negative shock (i.e., assets that have a positive beta to the market portfolio) should carry a positive risk premium—see, for example, Rubinstein (1976). However, riskless government bonds have countercyclical payoffs but have earned a positive average excess return. This reality is hard to reconcile with theory. It may be conjectured that nominal government bonds carried a positive risk premium for inflation risk for a long time, given the experience of the Great Inflation of 1965–1985. The success of monetary policy in taming inflation came as a surprise to the bond markets, and bonds continued to deliver positive excess returns. The liability- or consumption-hedging value of risk-free bonds was priced into the yield curve only in the late 1990s, after fears of runaway inflation had been definitively conquered.

In Chapter 5, we focus on the link between market valuation and risk premia. Since asset prices fall as expected risk premia increase and vice versa (holding all else constant), large variations in valuation metrics such as dividend yield and earnings yield (and their equivalents in the bond markets) should be indicative of significant changes in risk premia. We argue that the data broadly support this general conclusion. The excess volatility in financial markets makes it conceivable that value opportunities do appear from time to time, especially when the effects of negative economic news are compounded by sharp rises in demand for liquidity and immediacy. The challenge is to distinguish between value opportunities and value traps. (A value trap is an asset that appears cheap but is not.) Simple valuation metrics can help in this task. However, a mechanical implementation of such metrics may not work. One should use a portfolio of valuation metrics (rather than relying on only one) and assess the forces that might have caused the apparent value opportunity. Despite these difficulties, the basic logic of a value-driven investment style is compelling. A robust system for generating valuation metrics and intelligently analyzing them is critical to a long-term investment process.

In Chapter 6, we show how to combine the inputs of volatilities, correlations, and risk premia to construct an optimal portfolio of exposures to key global risk factors. We use the simple one-period mean–variance model for this purpose. We show that despite its simplicity, this approach can be fruitfully used to construct realistic portfolios. The key message is elementary but too often forgotten in practice: The optimal portfolio consists of a balance of procyclical and countercyclical exposures. A formal portfolio construction exercise, such as the one we consider, avoids doubling up on macro bets and tries to exploit relative value between correlated macro risk factors. This approach serves to avoid biases resulting from overconfidence in opinions about market outcomes, the predictability of which is typically much lower than is commonly thought. We also show how to bring considerations of tail risk into the optimization, permitting a differentiated treatment of risk factors that vary in their tail risk, such as equity returns and credit spreads.

Finally, we devote Chapter 7 to considerations that come into play when we include alternative assets (those beyond publicly traded stocks, bonds, and currencies) in the optimal portfolio. These assets include real estate, farmland, timber, infrastructure assets, and assets managed by specialist managers, such as hedge funds, private equity managers, and venture capitalists. These investments are illiquid, and transparency about the exact nature of the risks they entail is typically lacking. Investors must take special care in modeling the risk and factor exposures of these assets. We must explicitly account for the return smoothing that is often observed in the time series of returns on alternatives. The unsmoothed returns can then be mapped onto risk factors that drive traditional assets as well as onto idiosyncratic factors. We use this construct to compute realistic estimates of volatilities, correlations, and Sharpe ratios. These are the inputs to be used in portfolio construction exercises with alternative investments.

Our goal is to show how we apply existing research and its extensions to solve real-life portfolio allocation problems. We intend to convey the insights we have obtained from this amalgam of research and practice in numerous portfolio construction exercises. In our applications, we have found that a broad choice of models works best. Also, we prefer parsimonious and simple models over complex ones. We believe that simplicity and modularity lend substantial robustness to investment analysis.

The monograph is meant to be partly pedagogical, and it draws heavily on the vast body of knowledge that has been built by financial economists over the last 50 years. This research has led to significant advances in our understanding of risk factor decomposition of asset returns, determinants of risk and risk premia, and optimal portfolio choice. A detailed reference list of the literature on these topics would be too large to include in this monograph. Instead, we refer the reader to a selection of classics on asset pricing and portfolio choice: Back (2010); Cochrane (2005); Campbell, Lo, and McKinley (1996); Duffie (2002); Ilmanen (2011); Merton (1992); and Rubinstein (2006). We have also drawn extensively on what we have learned from our participation in PIMCO's investment process. We hope that students of investing in the financial industry as well as in academia will find our exposition useful.

2. Key Risk Factors in Bond and Equity Markets

The process of determining an optimal asset allocation can appear daunting in the face of the breadth and complexity of the universe of financial instruments. Equity portfolios can span a large number of sectors and countries. Fixed-income portfolios can include bonds of different maturities issued by entities with varying levels of credit risk and in different currencies. In addition to the traditional mix of publicly traded equity and debt, institutional portfolios include allocations to asset classes as diverse as private equity, private credit, venture capital, real estate, and infrastructure. We aim to demonstrate in this chapter, however, that the apparent complexity of the task of asset allocation can be addressed effectively if we focus on the exposure of asset classes to a relatively small set of risk factors. One can summarize a large part of the risk in even the most complex portfolios in terms of their exposures to a parsimonious set of systematic risk factors. Doing so allows investors to replace optimal *asset allocation* with optimal *risk factor allocation*—a much more tractable exercise. We can then focus on the optimal allocation of a risk budget to key risk factors rather than directly on a large menu of assets in financial markets.

In this chapter, we discuss the key risk factors for publicly traded bonds and equities. In Chapter 7, we show that alternative assets are exposed to the same set of risk factors that describe the behavior of bonds and equities.

2.1. Key Risk Factors for Bonds

We begin by considering the case of bonds. Bonds are conceptually simpler than equities because their promised cash flows are known more or less with certainty and most of their risk can therefore be attributed to variations in discount rates (interest rates). These discount rates have a time-to-maturity dimension and a credit risk dimension. The variations in both these components are governed by a small set of risk factors. We first focus on the default-free discount rates and then consider the risk factor characterization of credit spreads.

2.1.1. Characterizing the Variations in the Default-Free Yield Curve. For most countries, government bonds issued in their own currency effectively have no default risk in nominal terms. A typical riskless yield curve contains yields for a maturity spectrum that ranges from short maturities of

three to six months to maturities as long as 30 (or even 50) years. But we do not need to consider the risk of variations in yield of every maturity. There are two reasons for this: First, riskless rates of all maturities are impacted by the common macroeconomic forces of monetary policy, real growth, and expected inflation. Second, arbitrage ensures that bonds that are close substitutes trade at similar yields; hence, yields for bonds with similar maturities are highly correlated.

We can use principal components analysis (PCA)[1] to demonstrate that variations in riskless yields of various maturities can be explained by a small number of factors (that is, there is a low-dimensional representation of their dynamics). As documented in Litterman and Scheinkman (1991), most of the returns on any default-free government security or portfolio of such securities can be explained by just three factors: the level factor, the slope factor, and the curvature factor. The *level* factor represents parallel shifts in the yield curve. Bond yields of all maturities are affected by (or "load on") this factor roughly equally. The *slope* factor captures the changes in the steepness or slope of the yield curve, and it accounts for the fact that yields of different maturities do not always move in parallel. Finally, the *curvature* factor captures the movements of the "belly" of the yield curve relative to long and short maturities.

Below, we present the results of a PCA using a long time series of changes in US Treasury yields. **Exhibit 2.1** displays the exposures of the yield of each maturity to the first, second, and third principal components (PC1, PC2, and PC3, respectively), computed using the empirical covariance matrix of monthly changes in US Treasury yields from 1962 to 2015. As expected, yields of all maturities are nearly uniformly exposed to PC1. Shorter maturities have a negative exposure to PC2, and long maturities have a positive exposure. Finally, short- and long-maturity yields load negatively on PC3, while intermediate maturities load positively. The reported loadings justify the interpretation of these principal components as the "level," "slope," and "curvature" factors, as stated above.

---

[1]Principal components analysis is a statistical methodology useful for extracting the key drivers of a set of variables being studied. It reduces a collection of N variables (e.g., changes in riskless yields of N different maturities) to K factors (with K much smaller than N), where these factors (or principal components) capture most of the variation in the data. In particular, the first principal component (PC1) is a (normalized) linear combination of the N variables that has the maximum variance. The second principal component (PC2) is the (normalized) linear combination of the underlying data that has the maximum variance among all combinations that are uncorrelated with PC1, and so on. For a formal description, see Campbell, Lo, and McKinley (1996, ch. 6).

Exhibit 2.1. Exposures to First Three Principal Components of Monthly Changes in US Treasury Yields of Various Maturities, January 1962–December 2015

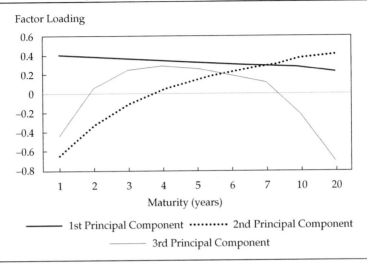

Notes: As of 31 December 2015. The above computations use monthly data. Monthly yield changes are computed using the dataset described in Gurkaynak, Sack, and Wright (2006) for the period 1962–2015, with two exceptions: 10-year yields are from the H.15 dataset of the Federal Reserve Board for January 1962–July 1971, and 20-year yields are from Ibbotson Associates' long-term government bond yields for the period January 1962–June 1981.

Sources: Federal Reserve; Gurkaynak, Sack, and Wright (2006); Ibbotson Associates; PIMCO.

Consistent with previous work, our analysis also confirms that the level factor explains over 93% of the variation in yield changes, slope contributes a non-negligible 6%, and curvature explains 1%. The remaining factors explain essentially 0%. **Exhibit 2.2** shows the proportion of variation explained by the principal components over rolling 5-year subsamples. It confirms that these results are reasonably stable over time.

Exhibit 2.2. Proportion of Variance of US Treasury Yield Changes Explained by Principal Components over Rolling 5-Year Subsamples, January 1967– December 2015

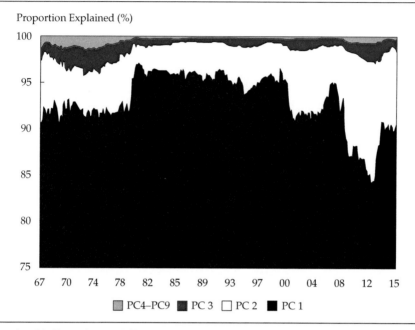

Notes: As of 31 December 2015. The above estimates use data on monthly yield changes, computed using the dataset described in Gurkaynak, Sack, and Wright (2006) for the period 1962–2015, with two exceptions: 10-year yields are from the H.15 dataset of the Federal Reserve Board for January 1962–July 1971, and 20-year yields are from Ibbotson Associates' long-term government bond yields for the period January 1962–June 1981.

Sources: Federal Reserve; Gurkaynak, Sack, and Wright (2006); Ibbotson Associates; PIMCO.

B2.1 Principal Components Analysis of the Default-Free Yield Curve: Global Evidence

We show below that the structure of principal components that we have documented for riskless yields in the United States also holds internationally. For easy comparability across markets, we use yields of interest rate swaps of various maturities as default-free yields. **Exhibit 2.3** shows the percentage of variance explained by the first three principal components of monthly swap yield changes in the United States, the euro area, Japan, and the United Kingdom.[2]

The percentages of variation explained by the three principal components are similar across regions. **Exhibit 2.4** shows that factor loadings are also broadly similar. The first factor affects all yields uniformly and is the level factor, while the second and third factors represent slope and curvature.

Exhibit 2.3. **Proportion of Variance of Swap Yield Changes Explained by Principal Components across Markets, January 1999–December 2015**

	US	UK	Euro Area	Japan
1st Principal Component	91%	87%	86%	85%
2nd Principal Component	8%	11%	12%	12%
3rd Principal Component	1%	1%	1%	2%
Other	0%	1%	0%	1%

Notes: As of 31 December 2015. These computations use monthly data.

Sources: Barclays; Bloomberg; PIMCO.

Note that Japan appears different from other regions in that slope factor (PC2) loadings are not strictly increasing over the entire maturity spectrum. The loadings are flat across the front end of the yield curve and then rise gradually from a maturity of five years onwards. This result is most likely due to the fact that Japan was in a zero interest rate environment throughout

---

[2]The analysis is based on changes in monthly swap rates for the following maturities: 2, 3, 4, 5, 7, 10, 15, 20, and 30 years. Our sample ranges from 1999 to 2015. All data were obtained from Bloomberg, with the exception of Japanese 30-year swap rates for January 1999– September 1999, which were obtained from Barclays Live.

Exhibit 2.4. **Exposures to First Three Principal Components of Monthly Changes in Swap Yields of Various Maturities, January 1999– December 2015**

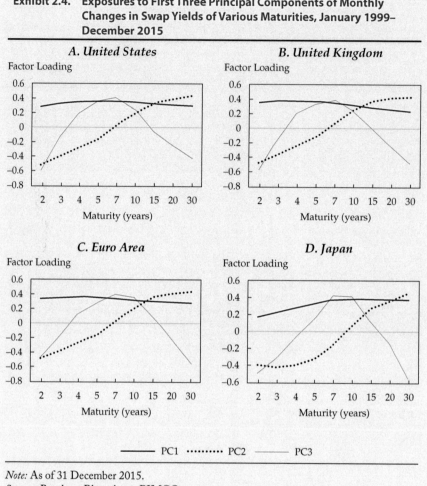

Note: As of 31 December 2015.
Sources: Barclays; Bloomberg; PIMCO.

this sample. As market participants expected that the zero interest rate policy would continue for a long time, all front-end yields got compressed near zero, their volatilities declined, and the slope of the yield curve in the front end was driven solely by the level of longer-term yields.

Interestingly, the impact of zero interest rate policies on yield curve dynamics is confirmed if we carry out a PCA of swap yields for the period 2010–2015, during which many central banks maintained a zero interest rate policy and engaged in quantitative easing. **Exhibit 2.5** shows that the factor loadings we obtain are qualitatively similar to the ones obtained for Japan

Exhibit 2.5. Exposures to First Three Principal Components of Monthly Changes in Swap Yields, January 2010–December 2015

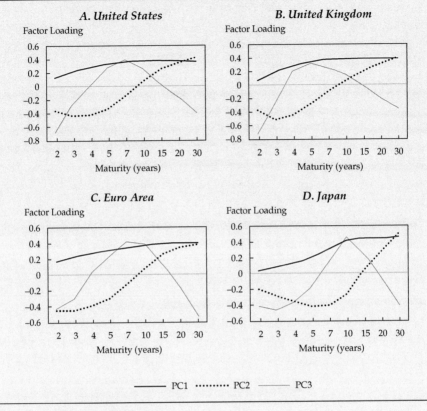

Note: As of 31 December 2015.
Sources: Barclays; Bloomberg; PIMCO.

for the period 1999–2015. It is also interesting to note that the peak of the loading to the first factor across regions in this sample period occurs at a maturity beyond five years (similar to the case of Japan in the full sample). Most likely, this result is also caused by the decline in volatility of short-maturity yields resulting from zero interest rate policies across the world in this sample.

▉ **Economic factors as drivers of the yield curve.** PCA derives the principal components purely statistically, as linear combinations of the underlying data. Also, the linear combination that describes the principal components can change over time. For making risk allocation decisions, therefore, it is often preferable to use a small number of *exactly identified* (named) and economically interpretable factors instead of "disembodied" principal components, whose interpretation can vary, as descriptors of yield curve movements. In the choice of named factors, it is useful to recognize that the yield curve is determined by two quantities: (1) the short-, medium-, and long-term expectations of the path of policy rates and (2) the term structure of risk premia for bearing interest rate risk. The path of policy rates in turn is governed by expectations of real growth and inflation in the economy. Therefore, we find it intuitive to use *changes* in the following four factors as key drivers of the yield curve:

- *The yield of short-maturity (say, 1-year) government bonds (or "1-year yield"):* The movements in this variable can be a proxy for changes in short-term interest rates, which are typically set by central banks in the conduct of monetary policy.

- *The 1-year yield one year forward less the 1-year yield:* The 1-year yield one year forward (hereafter, the 1-year × 1-year yield) is the rate that can be locked in today for riskless lending/borrowing one year from now for one year. This rate depends on the market expectation of the 1-year rate in one year's time and the risk premium for the risk of variations in short-term interest rates. The change in the differential between this forward rate and the 1-year yield is a proxy for the changes in the amount of policy tightening (or easing) priced into the front end of the yield curve. It is, thus, a good summary measure of the movements in the stance of monetary policy and in expectations of its near-term evolution. Since this factor is derived from market prices, it also embeds information about the variations in the risk premium associated with the risk of changes in monetary policy.

- *The 5-year yield five years forward less the 1-year yield:* The 5-year yield five years forward (hereafter, 5-year × 5-year yield) can be thought of as the rate that can be locked in today for riskless lending/borrowing for a term of five years five years from now. The variations in the differential between this yield and the 1-year yield are a proxy for changes in medium-term expectations of growth and inflation and the risk premium embedded in the belly of the yield curve (relative to the near-term expectations of these quantities). The advantage of using the 5-year × 5-year yield is that we incorporate information about growth and inflation expectations beyond the current monetary policy cycle.

- *The slope or difference between the 30-year yield and the 10-year yield:* This variable helps to capture the behavior of the long end of the yield curve, which likely is determined by clientele effects in addition to macroeconomic factors.

To depict the effectiveness of the above variables in capturing movements in the entire yield curve, we consider the following regression for the change in the riskless par yield for maturity of *n* years:

$$\Delta y(n) = \alpha + \beta_1 \Delta(\text{1-year yield})$$
$$+\beta_2 \Delta(\text{1-year} \times \text{1-year yield} - \text{1-year yield})$$
$$+\beta_3 \Delta(\text{5-year} \times \text{5-year yield} - \text{1-year yield})$$
$$+\beta_4 \Delta(\text{30-year - 10-year yield}) + \varepsilon.$$

Details of the regression equation used are in the Appendix (item A.2.1).

Exhibit 2.6 reports the estimates of $(\beta_1,\beta_2,\beta_3,\beta_4)$ for the above regression using data on US swap rates for the period January 1999 to December 2015.

The four factors mentioned above capture almost all the movements in US Treasury yields of various maturities. Regression R^2 ranges from 0.96 to 0.99. The beta exposures of various points on the yield curve are intuitive in magnitude and sign. The first factor (changes in the 1-year yield) serves as the level factor. All yields move essentially one for one with this factor. The effect of the second factor (changes in the 1-year × 1-year yield minus the 1-year yield), which we are interpreting as capturing shifts in the near-term path of policy rates and the associated risk premium, peaks at the 3-year point and declines steadily thereafter. The effect of the third factor (changes in the 5-year × 5-year yield minus the 1-year yield) increases steadily up to the 10-year point and stabilizes thereafter. The last factor (changes in the 30-year minus 10-year yield) has the most significant (and positive) loading on the longest maturities, as expected, while sensitivities of yields in the belly of the curve are negative. **Exhibit 2.7**, which repeats Exhibit 2.6 for a shorter and more recent period, shows that the general pattern of the betas for these factors remained more or less the same during the period of extraordinary monetary policy following the 2008 global financial crisis.

Of course, the ease of interpretation that comes with explicitly defined yield curve factors does come with some costs. The obvious cost is that we

Exhibit 2.6. Betas of Monthly Changes in US Swap Yields to Four Explicitly Defined Factors, January 1999–December 2015

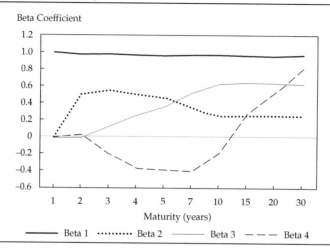

Notes: As of 31 December 2015. Beta 1 is a 1-year yield, Beta 2 is (1 year × 1-year yield − 1-year yield), Beta 3 is (5-year × 5-year yield − 1-year yield), and Beta 4 is (30-year yield − 10-year yield). *Sources:* Bloomberg; PIMCO.

Exhibit 2.7. Betas of Monthly Changes in US Swap Yields to Four Explicitly Defined Factors, January 2010–December 2015

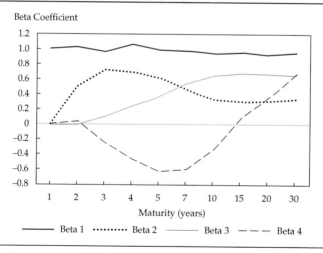

Notes: As of 31 December 2015. Beta 1 is a 1-year yield, Beta 2 is (1 year × 1-year yield − 1-year yield), Beta 3 is (5-year × 5-year yield − 1-year yield), and Beta 4 is (30-year yield − 10-year yield). *Sources:* Bloomberg; PIMCO.

need four (rather than three) factors to adequately define yield curve movements. Secondly, and perhaps more importantly, the factors we have used have nonzero correlations with each other, and these correlations could change over time (see **Exhibit 2.8** and **Exhibit 2.9**). Thus, in interpreting the effect of a given movement in one of the factors we have used, we need to account for the correlation of that movement with movements in the other factors. In contrast, principal components are uncorrelated in any given sample by construction.

Exhibit 2.8. Correlation Matrix of Explicitly Defined Yield Curve Factors, January 1999–December 2015

	1-Year Yield	1-Year × 1-Year Yield – 1-Year Yield	5-Year × 5-Year Yield – 1-Year Yield	30-Year Yield – 10-Year Yield
1-Year Yield	1.00	0.03	−0.38	−0.49
1-Year × 1-Year Yield – 1-Year Yield		1.00	0.53	−0.36
5-Year × 5-Year Yield – 1-Year Yield			1.00	0.15
30-Year Yield – 10-Year Yield				1.00

Notes: As of 31 December 2015. These computations use monthly data.
Sources: Bloomberg; PIMCO.

Exhibit 2.9. Correlation Matrix of Explicitly Defined Yield Curve Factors, January 2010–December 2015

	1-Year Yield	1-Year × 1-Year Yield – 1-Year Yield	5-Year × 5-Year Yield – 1-Year Yield	30-Year Yield – 10-Year Yield
1-Year Yield	1.00	0.21	−0.26	−0.39
1-Year × 1-Year Yield – 1-Year Yield		1.00	0.45	−0.47
5-Year × 5-Year Yield – 1-Year Yield			1.00	0.31
30-Year Yield – 10-Year Yield				1.00

Notes: As of 31 December 2015. These computations use monthly data.
Sources: Bloomberg; PIMCO.

Despite these shortcomings, we favor the approach that considers yield curve movements in terms of a few explicitly defined and economically interpretable factors. The fact that they are correlated is an advantage because it forces portfolio managers to think actively about the appropriate values of these correlations over their decision horizons. The correlations (and volatilities) of yield curve factors, such as short rates and slopes of the yield curve at different points, are influenced strongly by the stage of the business cycle and the expected stance of monetary policy. Consequently, in our analysis in later chapters, we use explicitly defined factors for allocation of the risk budget to interest rate risk.

2.1.2. Characterizing the Variations in Credit Spreads. Bonds that are free from default risk form only part of the universe of investable bonds. Only bonds issued by sovereign governments (issuing in their own currency) come close to being default-risk free. All other bonds embed credit risk in addition to interest rate risk. This distinction is a pillar of the risk factor approach to asset allocation with macroeconomic foundations. Thinking about the universe of bonds (e.g., the bonds included in broad fixed-income benchmarks, such as the Barclays Aggregate Bond Index) as a single asset class conflates interest rate risk and "spread" risk. (Spread risk is the risk of fluctuations in a bond's price due to non-interest-rate factors, the most important of which are related to default or credit risk.) By using the risk factor approach, we make each separate driver of return variation, with its own macroeconomic sensitivities, explicit. We thereby allow for distinct allocations to each of these sources of risk.

To characterize the dynamics of credit spreads, we study returns to corporate bonds in excess of a portfolio of otherwise similar risk-free bonds. This reference portfolio must be formed so that it matches the sensitivities of the credit-risky bond portfolio to changes in riskless yields at a few key maturity points (the so-called key rate durations). These differential returns of the two portfolios are referred to as *excess returns over risk-free bonds*. These *excess* returns are the portion of returns that is due to variations in the credit spread, not to changes in the default-free yield curve.

▨ *Common drivers of credit excess returns.* We seek to model credit excess returns on bonds issued by a variety of issuers in a low-dimensional way. In order to do this, we create a number of test portfolios of relatively homogeneous bonds. These test portfolios are value-weighted portfolios of bonds in the intersection of sector, rating, and maturity subdivisions of the Barclays US Corporate Index (a broad index of US investment-grade bonds) and the Barclays US Corporate High Yield Index (a broad index of US high-yield bonds). Sectors are financial and nonfinancial; ratings are Aaa/Aa combined, A, Baa, Ba, and B; and maturities are 1–5 years, 5–10 years, and greater than 10 years. See the Appendix (item A.2.2) for details of the dataset and the regression specifications used below.

▨ *Dominance of the market portfolio.* The first systematic factor that we consider is the movement in the credit spreads of the aggregate credit market. To document how large this common component is, we use the union of all corporate bonds in the Barclays US Corporate and US Corporate High Yield indices, excluding bonds with an index rating of Caa or worse (using Moody's nomenclature) as a proxy for the credit market portfolio.

We regress the normalized excess returns of our test portfolios on the normalized excess returns of the credit market portfolio, as follows:

Credit Model 1

$$\frac{\text{Excess return} \left(i^{th} \text{ test portfolio} \right)}{\text{Spread duration} (i) \times \text{Spread}(i)} = \alpha(i)$$

$$+ \beta(i) \frac{\text{Excess return (market portfolio)}}{\text{Spread duration (market)} \times \text{Spread(market)}} + \varepsilon.$$

Thus, the empirical results presented below are for a time series of the excess returns on a test portfolio, divided by the *spread duration of the portfolio times the credit spread of the portfolio.*

Spread duration (used in our specification above) is defined as the sensitivity of the bond price to changes in the credit spread of the bond. (For a fuller discussion of spread duration, see Leibowitz, Krasker, and Nozari 1990.) Over short time horizons, excess returns on a portfolio of credit-risky bonds are approximately equal to the negative of *spread duration* times the change in the spread of the portfolio. Hence, excess returns *per year of spread duration* are approximately equal to the negative of the change in the spread of the portfolio. In addition, as can be seen in the equation above, we specify the dynamics of credit excess returns by normalizing them not only by spread duration but also by the current level of spreads. Thus, our model effectively specifies a relationship between *proportional* changes in spreads of the test portfolio and spreads of the market portfolio. This adjustment (normalization by spread level in addition to spread duration) is informed by a particular feature of credit spread movements—namely, the strong dependence of the volatility of spread changes on the level of spreads. The volatility of credit excess returns is higher when spreads are high (reflecting the fact that higher fundamental risk leads to higher spreads and higher volatility of spread changes). In Chapter 3, we document this level dependence of the volatility of credit excess returns more comprehensively. Our specification ensures that the distribution of dependent and independent variables has nearly constant volatility over time (that is, the distribution is homoskedastic over time) and an application of the standard regression methodology is valid.

Exhibit 2.10 displays the average R^2 across regressions for various test portfolios. We use data on monthly excess returns in all our analyses. The market portfolio explains on average 70% of the variation in returns to the typical corporate bond test portfolio. It may be noted, however, that since the dependent variables are excess returns on portfolios of bonds and not on individual bonds, our regressions underestimate the level of idiosyncratic risk in credit excess returns.

Exhibit 2.10. Average R^2 of Regressions of Excess Returns of Buckets of the Credit Universe (per unit Spread duration × Spread) on Excess Returns of the Credit Index (per unit Duration × Spread), January 1990– December 2015

	R^2 (Model 1)
Market	0.69
By quality	
Investment Grade (IG)	0.69
High Yield (HY)	0.71
By sector	
Financials	0.68
Nonfinancials	0.70
By maturity	
1–5y	0.62
5–10y	0.79
10y+	0.68

Notes: As of 31 December 2015. These computations use monthly data on excess returns (over duration-matched Treasuries) on subindices of the Barclays Corporate Index and the Barclays Corporate High Yield Index. See the Appendix (item A.2.2) for details.
Sources: Barclays POINT; PIMCO.

Exhibit 2.11 displays the average univariate betas of credit rating portfolios[3] on the market portfolio under the regression described above. For comparison, we also report market betas from regressions using excess returns per year of spread duration (i.e., *without* division by current spread levels):

Credit Model 1A

$$\frac{\text{Excess return}\left(i^{th} \text{ test portfolio}\right)}{\text{Spread duration }(i)} = \alpha(i) + \beta(i)\frac{\text{Excess return (market portfolio)}}{\text{Spread duration (market)}} + \varepsilon.$$

Notice that the betas cluster close to 1 when excess returns are normalized by beginning-of-period spread levels, as they were in the first set of regressions. In contrast, betas vary dramatically across portfolios formed on credit rating when we do not normalize the data by spread levels and use only excess returns per year of duration, as we did in the second set. Of course, the primary driver of this result is the link between the volatility of spread changes and spread levels mentioned earlier. For example, the Aaa/Aa rated portfolios have a much lower average spread than the B rated portfolios (0.7% vs. 5.0%) because investors do not demand as high a spread over Treasuries for corporate bonds with a very low probability of default. This lower spread is associated with a much lower volatility of excess returns per unit of spread duration; the average volatility of excess returns per unit spread duration is just 0.4% per year for Aaa/Aa rated bonds versus 2.3% per year for B rated bonds. For this reason, in the regression using returns per unit spread duration, the market beta of the Aaa/Aa rated portfolio is just 0.5 whereas the market beta of the B rated portfolio is 2.4. Recall that the beta coefficient equals the correlation between the dependent and independent variables multiplied by *the ratio of their standard deviations*. In contrast, the market betas for these portfolios are close to 1 under the specification using excess returns normalized by spread duration times spread.

---

[3]The exhibit displays the equally weighted average of betas for all of the sector/rating/maturity test portfolios that fall within the specified rating category.

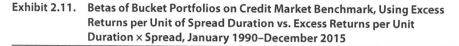

Exhibit 2.11. **Betas of Bucket Portfolios on Credit Market Benchmark, Using Excess Returns per Unit of Spread Duration vs. Excess Returns per Unit Duration × Spread, January 1990–December 2015**

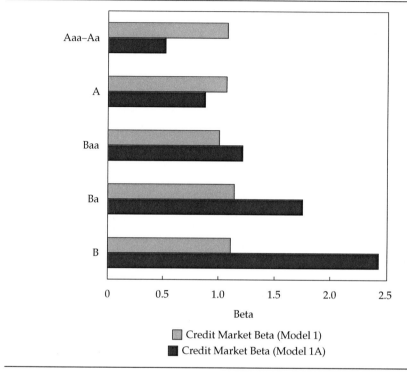

Notes: As of 31 December 2015. These computations use monthly data on excess returns (over duration-matched Treasuries) on subindices of the Barclays Corporate Index and the Barclays Corporate High Yield Index. Credit Model 1 refers to the regression in which both dependent and independent variables are normalized by spread duration times the spread of the portfolio. Credit Model 1A refers to the regression in which the normalization is done by dividing excess returns by spread duration only. See the Appendix (item A.2.2) for details.
Sources: Barclays POINT; PIMCO.

⬚ *Multifactor specifications.* While exposure to the market portfolio explains a large part of the variation in excess returns across issuers, Exhibit 2.10 shows that the fit of the single-factor model is not as good for some buckets as it is on average across buckets. In particular, the fit seems worse on average for short-maturity bonds: A credit *curve* factor seems to be present. We experiment with a multifactor specification below to gain insight into the contribution of this additional factor in explaining the cross section of credit excess returns.

The curve effect is incorporated by including, as an extra variable, the differential between (normalized) excess returns of a portfolio of short-maturity bonds and those of a portfolio of long-maturity bonds. The exact specification is provided in the Appendix (item A.2.2). The gain in the explanatory power from including the curve factor is apparent from **Exhibit 2.12**. The average R^2 increases to 73% for the regression that includes the curve factor from 70% for those that do not. The fit across maturity buckets is notably better.

Adding a sector-specific effect improves the explanatory power of the regressions further. To quantify the broad sector effect, we extend the above equation by including a factor that captures the outperformance of financial sector credits over nonfinancial credits, in addition to the market and curve factors.

The improvement from the inclusion of a broad sector effect is seen in the last column of Exhibit 2.12. The average R^2 across all buckets in our sample is 78% for the regression that incorporates sector as well as market and curve factors, and there are statistically significant gains in all buckets.

Exhibit 2.12. Average R^2 of Regressions of Excess Returns of Buckets of the Credit Universe (per unit Duration × Spread) on Market, Curve, and Sector Factors, January 1990–December 2015

	Market Factor	Market and Curve Factors	Market, Curve, and Sector Factors
Market	**0.69**	**0.73**	**0.78**
By quality			
Investment grade	0.69	0.72	0.78
High yield	0.71	0.74	0.78
By sector			
Financials	0.68	0.71	0.82
Nonfinancials	0.70	0.74	0.75
By maturity			
1–5 years	0.62	0.67	0.73
5–10 years	0.79	0.79	0.84
10+ years	0.68	0.72	0.76

Notes: As of 31 December 2015. These computations use monthly data on excess returns (over duration-matched Treasuries) on subindices of the Barclays Corporate Index and the Barclays Corporate High Yield Index. See the Appendix (item A.2.2) for details of the regression specification.
Sources: Barclays POINT; PIMCO.

The inclusion of a factor representing the outperformance of financial credits over nonfinancial credits allows the model to capture the behavior of credit markets during the 2008 global financial crisis and its aftermath, which is the main reason why the fit improves so notably. To the extent that financial and nonfinancial sectors could be influenced by different systematic economic drivers, this sector effect is a valuable one to incorporate into a model of credit returns.

2.2. Key Risk Factors for Equities

We have seen that a large part of the risk in fixed-income securities can be captured by three or four factors that govern interest rate movements and by a similar number of factors that capture variations in credit spreads. These factors were sufficient to explain more than 95% of the interest rate risk and 70%–80% of the spread risk of granular fixed-income portfolios. Is a similar decomposition possible for global equities? If so, what are the key risk factors? Just as in credit markets, a world market portfolio of equities will dominate less diversified subportfolios, but how much of the various risks of equities can be captured by a single index? What is the role of sectors, and what is the role of countries or regions, in this risk decomposition? While equities in a given country or region are affected by common monetary and fiscal policies, firms in certain sectors will be influenced by global trends in their industries no matter where they are domiciled. Sectors such as technology, major pharmaceuticals, energy, and commodities are much more global than banks, utilities, and retail. Is it possible to say whether the geographical effect or the sector effect dominates? These are some of the questions that we address in this section.

As above, we seek to understand how well the returns on concentrated portfolios can be explained by a parsimonious factor structure. We do so by relating the returns on subindices of a broad equity universe to returns on less granular portfolios. The concentrated portfolios in our analysis are the ones representing region-sector indices. We attempt to explain their returns using the world equity index, regional indices, and global sector indices. All returns in the analysis below are monthly returns, measured in the US dollar (USD). We use data on the MSCI family of equity indices. See the Appendix (item A.2.3) for details of the dataset and the regression specifications.

The Standard "Market Model." The first model that we estimate is the standard "market model" regression, which regresses the excess return (excess return over the short-term riskless rate)[4] of a subportfolio on the excess return of a world equity market benchmark.

In **Exhibit 2.13a** and **Exhibit 2.13b**, we see the average R^2 of the market model regressions (referenced below as Equity Model 1), where the average is taken over different sets of *region × sector* indices. The full sample average R^2 (i.e., average R^2 over all 66 regressions) is 42%, the average R^2 for all developed markets regressions is 44%, and the average R^2 for all of the emerging market indices in our sample is 39%. Thus, world equity market beta explains less than half of the variations in the returns of relatively homogeneous region-sector portfolios. Among developed markets, Europe ex United Kingdom has the highest proportion explained by the world market factor, followed by North America. For sector portfolios in Japan, the average R^2 for Model 1 is only 25%, confirming the existence of a nontrivial local effect in Japan. Among sectors, health care and utilities exhibit a poorer fit than

Exhibit 2.13a. Average R^2 (by Region) of Regressions of Region × Sector Index Returns on the Returns of the World Market Index, January 1995–December 2015

	Equity Model 1 (market model)
World (all region × sector pairs)	0.42
Developed markets	0.44
Emerging markets (EM)	0.39
North America	0.49
Europe ex UK	0.59
UK	0.42
Japan	0.25
EM Asia	0.41
EM Latin America	0.41
EM Europe	0.37

Notes: As of 31 December 2015. The computations reported here use data on monthly excess returns of various indices from the MSCI family of indices. Data and regression specifications are detailed in the Appendix (item A.2.3).
Sources: Bloomberg; MSCI; PIMCO.

---

[4]We use the terms "excess return over the short-term riskless rate (short rate)" and "excess returns over cash" interchangeably.

Exhibit 2.13b.   Average R^2 (by Sector) of Regressions of Region × Sector Index Returns on the Returns of the World Market Index, January 1995– December 2015

	Equity Model 1 (market only)
World (all region × sector pairs)	0.42
Consumer discretionary	0.63
Consumer staples	0.42
Energy	0.43
Financials	0.59
Health care	0.27
Industrials	0.62
Information technology	0.47
Materials	0.57
Telecom	0.42
Utilities	0.33

Notes: As of 31 December 2015. The computations reported here use data on monthly excess returns of various indices from the MSCI family of indices. Data and regression specifications are detailed in the Appendix (item A.2.3).
Sources: Bloomberg; MSCI; PIMCO.

others, suggesting that sector- or region-specific effects might play a prominent role in explaining variations in their returns.

Sector and Region Effects. In the "market model" (Equity Model 1) regressions, the proportion of variation in the returns of granular region-sector portfolios that is unexplained by their broad equity market beta is significant (55%–60%). This result suggests that region and sector effects are likely to be quite important. To quantify these effects, we augment the market model with broad sector factors (Equity Model 2A) and with regional factors (Equity Model 2B). We also estimate a model with both sector and region effects (Equity Model 3). In defining the sector factors, we use the sector return in excess of the return on the market index (i.e., the regressor is the outperformance of the relevant global sector over the overall market) to reduce the correlation between the independent variables. Regional factors are similarly defined as the outperformance of the relevant regional indices over the world benchmark.

The regression with a world market factor and broad sector factors produces a market beta and a sector beta for each portfolio. Similarly, the regression with a world market factor and regional factors produces a market beta and a regional beta. The encompassing model that includes both sector returns and regional returns produces a market beta, a sector beta, and a region beta for each portfolio.

Exhibit 2.14a and **Exhibit 2.14b** show that including sector effects increases the average R^2 from 42% to 55% while including regional effects increases the average R^2 to 61%. Thus, from an aggregate perspective, regional effects seem somewhat more important than sector or industry effects. For emerging markets and Japan, regional effects are much larger than sector effects. Outside of these two regions—that is, in North America and Europe—however, the regional effect is smaller than the sector effect.

Exhibit 2.14a. Average R^2 (by Region) of Regressions of Region × Sector Index Returns on the World Market Index, Regional Indices, and Global Sector Indices, January 1995–December 2015

	Equity Model 1 (market only)	Equity Model 2A (market and sector)	Equity Model 2B (market and region)	Equity Model 3 (market, sector, and region)
World (all region × sector pairs)	0.42	0.55	0.61	0.74
Developed markets	0.44	0.64	0.59	0.78
Emerging markets (EM)	0.39	0.43	0.65	0.67
North America	0.49	0.85	0.55	0.91
Europe ex UK	0.59	0.75	0.70	0.85
UK	0.42	0.63	0.53	0.71
Japan	0.25	0.34	0.58	0.67
EM Asia	0.41	0.45	0.70	0.74
EM Latin America	0.41	0.44	0.65	0.67
EM Europe	0.37	0.39	0.59	0.61

Notes: As of 31 December 2015. The computations reported here use data on monthly excess returns of various indices from the MSCI family of indices. Data and regression specifications are detailed in the Appendix (item A.2.3).
Sources: Bloomberg; MSCI; PIMCO.

Exhibit 2.14b.   Average R^2 (by Sector) of Regressions of Region × Sector Index Returns on the Returns of the World Market Index, Regional Indices, and Global Sector Indices, January 1995–December 2015

	Equity Model 1 (market only)	Equity Model 2A (market and sector)	Equity Model 2B (market and region)	Equity Model 3 (market, sector, and region)
World (all region × sector pairs)	0.42	0.55	0.61	0.74
Consumer discretionary	0.63	0.69	0.78	0.84
Consumer staples	0.42	0.64	0.59	0.79
Energy	0.43	0.70	0.58	0.80
Financials	0.59	0.68	0.82	0.91
Health care	0.27	0.50	0.39	0.56
Industrials	0.62	0.67	0.79	0.84
Information technology	0.47	0.62	0.56	0.68
Materials	0.57	0.75	0.74	0.87
Telecom	0.42	0.61	0.57	0.73
Utilities	0.33	0.54	0.50	0.67

Notes: As of 31 December 2015. The computations reported here use data on monthly excess returns of various indices from the MSCI family of indices. Data and regression specifications are detailed in the Appendix (item A.2.3).
Sources: Bloomberg; MSCI; PIMCO.

Recall also that all our returns are measured in US dollars and therefore will tend to overstate the country effect.

It is also interesting to compare the average R^2 for various sectors for Model 2A and Model 3 in Exhibit 2.14a. The incremental R^2 between these models measures the additional explanatory power contributed by regional effects. The sectors where regional effects are least important are information technology, health care, and energy. This result is intuitive as these sectors tend to be dominated by highly global companies, and in the case of energy, these firms are highly influenced by globally determined commodity prices. Interestingly, the financial and industrial sectors turn out to be sectors where regional effects make the greatest contribution.

Even Equity Model 3 leaves about a quarter of the return variation "unexplained" on average. Not surprisingly, a large idiosyncratic component is observed in Japanese and emerging market equities. For developed markets other than Japan, the idiosyncratic component is relatively modest: For North America, Model 3 leaves out as unexplained only 9% of return variation on average, and for Europe ex United Kingdom, the corresponding number is 15%.

Exhibit 2.15 shows the averages of betas (from Model 3) over various segments of the sample. All market betas are statistically significant. The average market beta is 0.97. (We do not expect the betas to average to exactly 1.0 because we use an equal-weighted average of the 66 market betas, one for each region-sector pair in our sample, instead of their market-weighted average.) Also, note that the larger a region's or sector's weight within the market portfolio, the more its beta should tend towards 1.0, holding everything else constant. Sector betas are smaller for Japan and emerging markets as their regional effects are particularly pronounced.

Our results are related to those documented by Heston and Rouwenhorst (1995). These authors analyzed the returns on 829 individual firms in 12 different European countries (belonging to 7 different industries). They documented that country effects were larger than industry effects—almost

Exhibit 2.15. **Average Betas (by Region) from Regressions of Region × Sector Index Returns on the Returns of the World Market Index, Regional Indices, and Global Sector Indices (Equity Model 3), January 1995–December 2015**

	Beta 1	Beta 2	Beta 3
World (all region × sector pairs)	0.97	0.70	0.88
Developed markets	0.99	0.91	0.89
Emerging markets (EM)	0.94	0.41	0.88
North America	0.99	1.17	0.89
Europe ex UK	1.03	0.85	0.90
UK	1.02	0.94	0.80
Japan	0.94	0.68	0.96
EM Asia	0.94	0.50	0.89
EM Latin America	0.86	0.34	0.87
EM Europe	1.00	0.40	0.88

Notes: As of 31 December 2015. The computations reported here use data on monthly excess returns of various indices from the MSCI family of indices. Data and regression specifications are detailed in the Appendix (item A.2.3).
Sources: Bloomberg; MSCI; PIMCO.

twice as large. Our findings in Exhibit 2.14a show that the dominance of the country/region effect is much weaker in our sample and is largely concentrated in emerging markets and Japan. When we use a methodology similar to these authors' on our dataset, we find that the time-series standard deviation of country effects is about 33% larger than that of sector effects. Note that our sample period is more recent and covers many more geographical areas. As mentioned before, the fact that we use returns denominated in a single currency (USD) in our analysis—similar to Heston and Rouwenhorst, who used the German mark (DEM)—is likely to exaggerate the country effect in some cases.

Overall, the above results suggest that a high-level representation of equity markets can begin with a world equity index and then incorporate a small number of regional and global sector tilts. This approach would capture about 75% of the variation present in equity returns of region-sector portfolios. It should, however, be noted that the part of equity returns that is attributable to factors other than the world market portfolio, global sectors, and geographic locations is not trivial. Indeed, 75% is likely to be an overestimate of the size of the systematic component in equities because we are using portfolio returns as our dependent variables instead of returns on individual stocks.

2.3. Currencies as Risk Factors in Global Portfolios

We have so far characterized the risk structure of returns on bonds and equities without particular consideration to the domicile of the investor and the assets held. For global investors who hold assets denominated in currencies other than their base currencies, we must also consider currency risk. All foreign assets come with currency exposures that affect total volatility unless currency risk has been fully hedged. Consider the case of a US investor who invests in the UK stock market. The return the investor receives equals the return experienced by a UK investor in her local stock market plus (minus) appreciation (depreciation) in the price of British pounds (GBP) as stated in US dollars. Risk in the exchange rate component can contribute substantially to overall risk in the position.

Exhibit 2.16 shows the relative importance of currency volatility in equity and fixed-income portfolios. It compares volatilities of US dollar and local currency total returns of various equity and fixed-income indices. Exhibit 2.16 also shows the volatility of changes in spot exchange rates and the correlations between changes in exchange rates and the local currency total returns. The variance of the US dollar total returns of an index equals the sum of the variance of local currency returns, the variance of changes in

Exhibit 2.16. Volatilities of Equity, Fixed-Income, and Currency Returns and Correlations between Currency Movements and Local Returns on Equities and Bonds, January 1999–December 2015

	Volatilities (% per year)			
Equity Markets (MSCI)	USD Total Return	Local Currency Return	% Δ in Spot FX	Correlation (% Δ in FX, Local Currency Return)
USA	15%	15%	0%	—
UK	17	14	9	4%
France	22	18	10	13
Germany	25	22	10	10
Japan	17	18	10	−35
Spain	25	21	10	22
Australia	22	13	13	48
Canada	21	15	9	50
Switzerland	16	14	11	−13
Hong Kong	22	22	0.44	10
Denmark	21	18	10	0
China	31	31	0.43	12
Korea	32	27	11	36
Taiwan	27	25	5	42
Brazil	33	21	16	53
South Africa	26	18	16	14
India	31	27	8	46
Russia	41	38	7	27
Mexico	25	20	9	35
Malaysia	22	14	16	8
Indonesia	38	28	15	47

(continued)

Exhibit 2.16. Volatilities of Equity, Fixed-Income, and Currency Returns and Correlations between Currency Movements and Local Returns on Equities and Bonds, January 1999–December 2015 (continued)

Equity Markets (MSCI)	Volatilities (% per year)			Correlation (% Δ in FX, Local Currency Return)
	USD Total Return	Local Currency Return	% Δ in Spot FX	
Thailand	33	29	6	54
Fixed-Income Indices				
Barclays Euro Aggregate	11%	3%	10%	2%
Barclays Global Aggregate	6	3	4	22
Barclays Global Treasury	7	3	6	17
JPM GBI-EM Global Diversified	12	5	9	54

Notes: As of 31 December 2015. Equity returns are based on MSCI country-level total return (net) indices and include dividends net of withholding taxes. Currency (FX) volatility is calculated by computing the annualized standard deviation of the difference between local currency returns and (unhedged) US dollar returns of regional equity and fixed-income indices. For global fixed-income indices denominated in US dollars, currency volatility is estimated using the difference between the unhedged index return and the US-dollar-hedged return. All data are at monthly frequency, from January 1999 to December 2015, except for the JP Morgan Government Bond Index-Emerging Markets Global Diversified Index, which uses data from January 2003 to December 2015.

the spot foreign exchange (FX) rate, and the covariance term. The values reported in this exhibit clarify the relative contribution of each of these terms to the volatility of US dollar total returns.

Exhibit 2.16 shows that the currency volatility in unhedged equity portfolios is of the same order of magnitude (broadly speaking) as the volatility of local currency returns in the underlying indices. However, currency volatility in unhedged fixed-income indices dwarfs the volatility of local currency (or US-dollar-hedged) returns.

Exhibit 2.16 also shows that currency fluctuations are not independent of other factors, such as interest rate changes and equity returns. It is necessary to take account of these correlations in the construction of an optimal risk–reward trade-off. High-interest-rate currencies, such as the Australian dollar and various emerging market currencies, tend to correlate positively with stock market exposures, while low-interest-rate currencies, such as the Japanese yen, exhibit the opposite behavior. On the other hand, US-dollar-hedged returns on key global fixed-income indices are positively correlated with currency returns (and hence negatively correlated with the US dollar).

This correlation is especially pronounced in the case of emerging market bonds. Emerging markets' debt, equities, and currencies all tend to rally or decline together.

Many investors analyze currency risk with a view to determining an optimal currency-hedging strategy. However, the question of how much currency risk should be hedged is better posed within the context of the overall portfolio. An unconstrained global asset allocation exercise views currencies as sources of risk and risk premia. Since global currency markets are liquid and currency exposures can be managed directly, we do not need to conflate this risk with other risks in the portfolio. We can make an explicit allocation in the overall risk budget to currency risk as well as to equity, interest rate, and credit risks. This is the approach we take in our formulation of the top-down asset allocation problem.

Systematic Factors in Currency Markets. It is also useful in this context to assess sources of systematic variation in currency returns. We begin with a simple principal components decomposition of the covariance matrix

Exhibit 2.17. Exposures to the First Two Principal Components of Developed Market Currency Returns vs. US Dollar, January 1999–December 2015

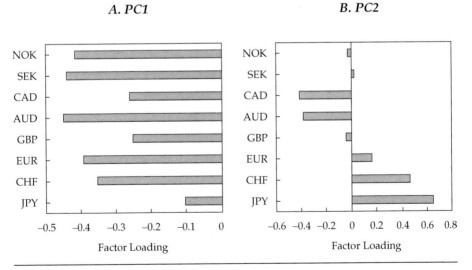

Notes: As of 31 December 2015. The above computations use monthly excess returns on various currencies. Excess returns on a currency are defined as the sum of spot returns (of the foreign currency vs. the US dollar) and the interest rate differential. These excess returns are computed using 1-month forwards, held to expiration.
Sources: Bloomberg; PIMCO.

of monthly excess returns (in US dollars) on a number of developed market currencies. The results are shown in **Exhibit 2.17.**

The first two principal components explain 66% and 12%, respectively, of the variation in returns across currencies over the past 17 years. The exposures of currencies to these principal components reveal interesting patterns. The first principal component appears to be a broad US dollar factor; all currencies have negative exposures to this factor. This finding might partially derive from the fact that the exchange rates in this experiment are versus the US dollar. However, this result is consistent with the dominant role played by the US dollar in bilateral exchange rate markets due to its status as a reserve currency.

The second principal component has opposite signs on the exposures of low-interest-rate currencies, such as the Japanese yen and the Swiss franc, and high-interest-rate currencies, such as the Australian dollar. In this way, it resembles a "currency carry trade" factor—widely known to be a systematic factor in currency markets. The large exposures of such currencies as the Australian dollar, the Canadian dollar, and the Norwegian krone to both principal components also potentially reflects a factor driven by commodity prices.

As we discussed above, in our analysis of the drivers of government bond yields, we generally prefer to work with "named" factors rather than latent ones (such as principal components) because it is easier to model the economic drivers of named factors. To this end, we examine the relationship between the first two principal components of currency returns and the three economically defensible drivers of currency returns: changes in the US dollar exchange rate versus a broad basket of currencies, returns of the currency "carry" trade (which is long high-interest-rate currencies and short low-interest-rate currencies), and returns of a broad commodity

Exhibit 2.18. Regression of PC1 and PC2 Returns on Named Factors, January 1999–December 2015

	Beta to Currency Carry	Beta to USD	Beta to Commodities	R^2
PC1	−0.3	−2.5	−0.6	57%
PC2	−1.2	0.4	*0.0*	53%

Notes: As of 31 December 2015. Estimates that are not statistically significant at the 1% level are italicized. These computations use monthly data on the two principal components and three named factors. See Appendix (item A.2.4) for details.
Sources: Bloomberg; PIMCO.

index. See Appendix (item A.2.4) for details. **Exhibit 2.18** presents the results of this analysis.

As one would expect from the exposures presented in Exhibit 2.17, the first two principal components have statistically significant exposures to factors that we consider in most cases. These results and observations are in line with Verdelhan (2015), which provides a risk-based explanation for why the currency carry and US dollar factors ought to explain variations in currency returns. However, it is worth noting that these factors explain only about 55% of the variation in the returns of these principal components.

Exhibit 2.19. Results of Regression of Developed Market Currency Returns (vs. US Dollar) on Carry, US Dollar, and Commodity Factors, January 1999–December 2015

	JPY	CHF	EUR	GBP	AUD	CAD	SEK	NOK
Beta to the currency carry factor	−0.8	−0.4	0.0	*0.1*	*0.8*	0.4	*0.0*	*0.1*
Beta to the dollar factor	0.6	1.0	1.1	1.0	0.8	0.6	1.1	1.0
Beta to the commodity factor	0.1	0.2	0.2	0.1	0.3	0.2	0.3	0.3
R^2	29%	28%	40%	44%	65%	48%	44%	46%

Notes: JPY is Japanese yen, CHF is Swiss franc, EUR is euro, GBP is British pound, AUD is Australian dollar, CAD is Canadian dollar, SEK is Swedish krona, and NOK is Norwegian krone. As of 31 December 2015. Estimates that are not statistically significant at the 1% level are italicized. These computations use monthly data on excess returns on various currencies and the named factors. See Appendix (item A.2.4) for details.
Sources: Bloomberg; PIMCO.

Exhibit 2.20. Results of Regression of Emerging Market Currency Returns (vs. US Dollar) on Carry, US Dollar, and Commodity Factors, January 2002–December 2015

	MXN	BRL	INR	TRY	PLZ
Beta to the currency carry factor	0.3	1.3	0.2	1.2	0.2
Beta to the dollar factor	0.8	0.7	0.6	0.7	1.2
Beta to the commodity factor	0.1	0.1	*0.1*	*0.1*	0.3
R^2	40%	50%	27%	54%	47%

Notes: MXN is Mexican peso, BRL is Brazilian real, INR is Indian rupee, TRY is Turkish lira, and PLZ is Polish zloty. As of 31 December 2015. Estimates that are not statistically significant at the 1% level are italicized. These computations use monthly data on excess returns on various currencies and the named factors. See Appendix (item A.2.4) for details.
Sources: Bloomberg; PIMCO.

In order to quantify the effectiveness of these named factors in directly explaining variations in currency returns, we regress currency returns on the "carry," "dollar," and "commodity" factors mentioned above. **Exhibit 2.19** and **Exhibit 2.20** present results of this regression for developed and emerging market currencies, respectively. The currency carry factors we use in the developed and emerging market regressions are constructed within the developed and emerging market universes of currencies, respectively.

We find that the three factors considered explain roughly 40% of the variation in developed market currency returns on average. All currencies load on the dollar and commodity factors, while exposures to the carry factor are more mixed.

The three factors explain a similar proportion (roughly 40%) of the variance of emerging market currencies on average, as we show in Exhibit 2.20.

2.4. A Short List of Risk Factors for a Top-Down Asset Allocation Exercise

We have shown that it is possible to construct a low-dimensional representation of the financial risks in the most important segments of investable assets, namely, publicly traded debt and equity. By putting together the major risk factors across global markets that we have identified, we arrive at a schema such as that shown in **Exhibit 2.21**. This schema can be used as a guide for a top-down global multi-asset optimal allocation exercise. In Chapter 6, we use a similar top-level factor set to illustrate how to implement such an exercise.

Exhibit 2.21. A Short List of Risk Factors for a Global Asset Allocation Exercise

Risk Category	Risk Factors	Markets	Representative Instruments
Interest rate risk	1. Front-end rates 2. 5-year x 5-year forwards 3. 30-year – 10-year yields	US, euro area, UK, Japan, Canada, Australia	1. Interest rate futures, 5-year and 10-year govt. bonds 2. bond futures, interest rate swaps 3. 10-year and 30-year govt. bonds, bond futures
Credit spread risk	1. Investment–grade (IG) credit spreads 2. High-yield (HY) credit spreads	US, euro area	1. Basket of liquid IG and HY bonds 2. IG and HY CDX contracts 3. Index-replicating ETFs
Equity risk	1. Return on the world market portfolio 2. Regional outperformance over world market 3. Sector outperformance over world market	1. Global developed and emerging markets (DM and EM) 2. North America, UK, Europe, Japan 3. Major EM blocks	1. Index futures 2. Country and global sector ETFs
Currency risk	1. Currency returns	Major DM and EM currencies	1. Currency forwards

Note: ETF = exchange-traded fund, DM = developed market, EM = emerging market, CDX = credit default swap.

35

Appendix A.2.

A.2.1. Regression of Change in Swap Yields on Named Factors (Results in Exhibit 2.6)
Exhibit 2.6 reports the results of the following regression:

$$\Delta y(t,n) = \alpha + \beta_1(n)\Delta y(t,1) + \beta_2(n)\Delta\big[y_f(t,1,1) - y(t,1)\big]$$
$$+ \beta_3(n)\Delta\big[y_f(t,5,5) - y(t,1)\big] + \beta_4(n)\Delta\big[y(t,30) - y(t,10)\big] + \varepsilon(t+1),$$

where $t = 0,1,\ldots,T-1$, T is the sample size, $y(t,n)$ denotes the (spot) yield to maturity on a default-risk-free par bond with n years to maturity at date t, $y_f(t,n,m)$ denotes the m-year forward par yield for n years to maturity at date t, $\Delta y(t,.)$ and $[\Delta y_f(t,.)]$ denote the changes in the respective yields between dates t and $t+1$, and $\{\varepsilon(t), t = 1,2,\ldots,T\}$ are regression error terms, assumed to satisfy the conditions required for the application of classical ordinary least squares regression (henceforth, "the usual conditions"). We use monthly data on US swap yields for these regressions.

A.2.2. Regressions for Credit Excess Returns (Results in Exhibits 2.10–2.12)

■ *Data.* The regressions results reported in Exhibits 2.10–2.12 use excess returns (over duration-matched Treasuries) of a number of relatively homogeneous test portfolios of US corporate bonds. These test portfolios are value-weighted portfolios of bonds in the intersection of sector, rating, and maturity subdivisions of the Barclays US Corporate Index (a broad index of US investment-grade bonds) and the Barclays US Corporate High Yield Index (a broad index of high-yield US bonds). Sectors are financial and non-financial; ratings are Aaa/Aa combined, A, Baa, Ba, and B; and maturities are 1–5 years, 5–10 years, and greater than 10 years.

Excluding sparsely populated sector × rating × maturity buckets leaves a total of 23 test portfolios. BB and B rated financials and AAA/AA rated financials (with 10+ years to maturity) are excluded because of lack of data. We focus on monthly data for the time period from January 1990 to December 2015, based on data availability. The numbers of portfolio constituents change over time, but on average, there are 185 bonds per portfolio, with a minimum of 35 bonds for "Nonfinancial B 10y+" and a maximum of 399 bonds for "Nonfinancial BBB 5–10y."

■ *Regression Specifications.* First, excess returns on bond i from date t to $t + 1$ (*per unit of spread duration*) are denoted by $R_{per\_dur}(i,t,t + 1)$. That is, $R_{per\_dur}(i,t,t + 1) = R(i,t,t + 1) / SD(i,t)$, where $SD(i,t)$ is the spread duration of the bond and $R(i,t,t + 1)$ is defined as $R(i,t,t + 1) = TR(i,t,t + 1) - TR_{RL}(i,t,t + 1)$, where $TR(i,t,t + 1)$ is the total return on bond i from t to $t + 1$ and $TR_{RL}(i,t,t + 1)$ is the total return on a portfolio of *riskless* bonds that has the same profile of interest rate sensitivities (key rate durations) as bond i. The excess return on a portfolio of bonds is defined similarly. As discussed in Section 2.1.2 of this chapter, our regression specifications use $R_{per\_dur}(i,t,t + 1)$ but with one more normalization. We divide $R_{per\_dur}(i,t,t + 1)$ in our regressions by the spread level of bond (or portfolio) i to ensure that the volatility of our dependent and independent variables is constant over time.

To be precise, the results reported in Exhibits 2.10–2.12 are for the following regression specifications:

Credit Model 1

$$\frac{R_{per\_dur}(i,t,t + 1)}{S(i,t)} = \alpha(i) + \beta(i)\frac{R_{per\_dur}(m,t,t + 1)}{S(m,t)} + \varepsilon(i,t + 1)$$

$$\text{for } i \in (sector) \times (rating) \times (maturity), t = 0,\ldots,T - 1,$$

where $R_{per\_dur}(i,t,t + 1)$ is the excess return (per year of spread duration) on the ith bucket of corporate bonds formed on sector-rating-maturity splits and $R(m,t,t + 1)$ is the excess return (per unit of spread duration) for the broad credit market portfolio. Moreover, $S(i,t)$ corresponds to the date t value-weighted average credit spread of bucket i, while $S(m,t)$ corresponds to the value-weighted average credit spread of the credit market portfolio.

The parameter $\beta(i)$ measures the beta of the ith bucket in the sample to the overall credit market return, and $\alpha(i)$ is the intercept. Additionally, $\{\varepsilon(i,t), t = 1,2,\ldots,T\}$ are the regression residuals, which are assumed to satisfy the usual conditions.

Credit Model 1A

$$R_{per\_dur}(i,t,t + 1) = \alpha(i) + \beta(i)R_{per\_dur}(m,t,t + 1) + \varepsilon(i,t)$$

$$\text{for } i \in (sector) \times (rating) \times (maturity), t = 0,\ldots,T - 1,$$

where all quantities are as defined previously.

Credit Model with Market and Curve Factors

$$\frac{R_{per\_dur}(i,t,t+1)}{S(i,t)} = \alpha(i) + \beta(i)\frac{R_{per\_dur}(m,t,t+1)}{S(m,t)}$$

$$+ \gamma(i)\left[\frac{R_{per\_dur}(s_{mat},t,t+1)}{S(s_{mat},t)} - \frac{R_{per\_dur}(\iota_{mat},t,t+1)}{S(\iota_{mat},t)}\right]$$

$$+ \varepsilon(i,t+1)$$

for $i \in (sector) \times (rating) \times (maturity), t = 0,\ldots,T-1,$

where $R_{per\_dur}(s_{mat},t,t+1)$ denotes the excess returns (per year of spread duration) of the value-weighted portfolio of all buckets of bonds in our sample with maturity of 1–5 years, while $R_{per\_dur}(\iota_{mat},t,t+1)$ denotes the excess returns per year of spread duration of the value-weighted portfolio of all buckets of bonds in our sample with maturity greater than 10 years. Beginning-of-period spread levels, $S(s_{mat},t)$ and $S(\iota_{mat},t)$, are defined similarly. All other quantities are as defined previously.

Credit Model with Market, Curve, and Sector Factors

$$\frac{R_{per\_dur}(i,t,t+1)}{S(i,t)} = \alpha(i) + \beta(i)\frac{R_{per\_dur}(m,t,t+1)}{S(m,t)}$$

$$+ \gamma(i)\left[\frac{R_{per\_dur}(s_{mat},t,t+1)}{S(s_{mat},t)} - \frac{R_{per\_dur}(\iota_{mat},t,t+1)}{S(\iota_{mat},t)}\right]$$

$$+ \theta(i)\left[\frac{R_{per\_dur}(fin,t,t+1)}{S(fin,t)} - \frac{R_{per\_dur}(nfin,t,t+1)}{S(nfin,t)}\right]$$

$$+ \varepsilon(i,t+1)$$

for $i \in (sector) \times (rating) \times (maturity), t = 0,\ldots,T-1,$

where $R_{per\_dur}(a,t,t+1)$ for $a = fin,nfin$ denotes excess returns (per unit of spread duration) of bonds of issuers in the financial and nonfinancial sectors, respectively. Beginning-of-period spread levels, $S(a,t), = fin,nfin$, are defined similarly. Other variables are as defined previously.

A.2.3. Regression for Equity Returns (Results in Exhibits 2.13a–2.15)

■ *Data.* For all regression results for equity returns (reported in Exhibits 2.13a–2.15), we use returns on the MSCI family of indices. The world equity index is represented by the MSCI ACWI Index. The 10 sectors we consider are the following GICS Level 1 sectors: materials, energy, industrials, information technology, consumer staples, consumer durables, financials, telecom services, utilities, and health care. The seven regions we consider are North America, Europe ex United Kingdom, United Kingdom, Japan, Emerging Markets (EM) Asia, Emerging Markets (EM) Latin America, and Emerging Markets (EM) Europe. Thus, in all, we have 70 region-sector pairs, from which we exclude 4 pairs because of irregular data availability, so our empirical analysis contains 66 region-sector pairs. The excluded pairs are EM Latin America Information Technology, EM Latin America Health Care, EM Europe Information Technology, and EM Europe Health Care. All returns are monthly returns measured in US dollars, and the short-term riskless rate is the US dollar short-term riskless rate. The sample period is January 1995–December 2015.

■ *Regression Specifications.* The model with the world equity market factor alone is the following:

Equity Model 1

$$\left[R(i,j,t+1) - r_f(t)\right] = \alpha(i,j) + \beta_1(i,j)\left[R_{market}(t+1) - r_f(t)\right] + \varepsilon(i,j,t+1)$$
$$\text{for } 1 \le i \le N_s(j), 1 \le j \le N_R, t = 1,2...,T-1,$$

where $R(i,j,t)$ denotes the total return at the end of month t on the index representing a value-weighted portfolio of equities of firms in sector i and region j, $N_s(j)$ denotes the number of sectors in the sample for region j, and N_R denotes the number of regions in the sample. Moreover, $R_{market}(t)$ is the total return on an index representing the world market portfolio; $r_f(t)$ is the riskless rate at the beginning of the period; $\alpha(i,j)$ is the intercept of the regression; $\beta_1(i,j)$ is the equity market beta; and $\varepsilon(i,j,t)$ is the error term that is assumed to satisfy the usual conditions. All returns are in US dollars, and $r_f(t)$ is the US dollar short-term riskless rate at the end of month t.

The model with a world market factor and broad sector factors is as follows:

Equity Model 2A

$$\left[R(i,j,t) - r_f(t-1)\right] = \alpha + \beta_1(i,j)\left[R_{market}(t) - r_f(t-1)\right]$$
$$+ \beta_2(i,j)\left[R_{sector}(i,t) - R_{market}(t)\right] + \varepsilon(i,j,t),$$

where $\beta_2(i,j)$ is the sector coefficient ("sector beta") of the portfolio of equities in the equity index for sector i and region j and $R_{sector}(i,t)$ denotes the return on the index of the ith global sector. All other variables are as defined for Model 1.

The model with a world market factor and regional factors is as follows:

Equity Model 2B

$$\left[R(i,j,t) - r_f(t-1)\right] = \alpha + \beta_1(i,j)\left[R_{market}(t) - r_f(t-1)\right]$$
$$+ \beta_2(i,j)\left[R_{region}(j,t) - R_{market}(t)\right] + \varepsilon(i,t),$$

where $\beta_2(i,j)$ is the region coefficient ("region beta") of the portfolio of equities in the equity index for sector i and region j and $R_{region}(j,t)$ denotes the total return on the equity index of the jth region. All other variables are as defined above.

Furthermore, the encompassing model with both sector and regional effects is as follows:

Equity Model 3

$$\left[R(i,j,t) - r_f(t-1)\right] = \alpha + \beta_1(i,j)\left[R_{market}(t) - r_f(t-1)\right]$$
$$+ \beta_2(i,j)\left[R_{sector}(i,t) - R_{market}(t)\right]$$
$$+ \beta_3(i,j)\left[R_{region}(j,t) - R_{market}(t)\right] + \varepsilon(i,j,t),$$

where $\beta_3(i,j)$ is the sector coefficient ("sector beta") of the portfolio of equities for sector i and region j.

A.2.4. Regression for Currency Returns (Results in Exhibits 2.18–2.20) For these results, we postulate that

$$r^{FX}(i,t) = \alpha_i + \beta_i r^{carry}(t) + \gamma_i r^{USD}(t) + \theta_i r^{commodity}(t) + \varepsilon(i,t),$$

where $r^{FX}(i,t)$ denotes the excess returns of the ith principal component (for results reported in Exhibit 2.18) or excess returns on currency i (versus the US dollar; for results reported in Exhibits 2.19 and 2.20). Moreover, $r^{carry}(t)$ denotes the FX carry factor, $r^{USD}(t)$ is the return of the US dollar spot versus a large group of major US trading partners (published by the Federal Reserve), and $r^{commodity}(t)$ denotes the returns of the Bloomberg Commodity Index. The FX carry factor represents the excess returns of a strategy that goes long high-interest-rate currencies and short low-interest-rate currencies. The developed markets FX carry factor goes long the top four and short the bottom four of the major developed market currencies (AUD, CAD, CHF, EUR, GBP, JPY, NOK, NZD [the New Zealand Dollar], and SEK). The EM FX carry factor is constructed in a universe of 9 major emerging market currencies (IDR, ILS, INR, KRW, MYR, PHP, RUB, SGD, and TWD) and goes long the top four and short the bottom four based on interest rates implied in 1-month FX forwards. The parameters β_i, γ_i, and θ_i denote the exposure of currency i to the above three factors, and $\varepsilon(i,t)$ are regression error terms.

3. Risk Factor Volatilities and Correlations and Their Macroeconomic Determinants

In the previous chapter, we showed how to create a parsimonious set of risk factors that captures a dominant portion of the risk in asset markets. Using this core set of risk factors, we can convert the seemingly impossible task of building a portfolio out of all the available assets in the world into a simpler exercise of choosing the optimal exposure to each of these risk factors rather than to a large number of assets. The next task in building an asset allocation framework is to develop useful estimates of risk and expected returns for key risk factors. This is the subject of our analysis in the next three chapters. In this chapter, we focus on the risk dimension. We present insights from an examination of the empirical properties of risk factor volatilities and correlations, in particular their link with the macroeconomy. These insights are useful for determining the volatility and correlation inputs to a portfolio construction exercise that is macro aware.

We begin with the observation that financial market volatility far exceeds most estimates of the volatility of economic fundamentals—such as GDP growth, earnings growth, and inflation—potentially reflecting overreaction in asset prices. We present evidence that volatility does not remain constant over time. Of particular interest to us is the dependence of asset return volatility on the stage of the business cycle. Financial market volatility is strongly countercyclical; that is, it is higher in economic downturns. In fixed-income markets (particularly credit markets), there is robust evidence that the volatility of credit returns is dependent on the level of credit spreads, with higher volatility when the spread is large. Finally, there is evidence of short-term reversals and medium-term persistence in volatility. Large shocks to volatility reverse partially in the short term, but a part of their effect is long lasting. All these properties of the empirical behavior of volatility in financial markets are important for macro-aware asset allocation.

We document also the fact that correlations, not just volatilities, are time varying and sensitive to the economic cycle. In particular, correlations become more extreme in recessions. "Risk-on" assets (such as equities and credit, which generally perform well when the economy is expanding) tend to become more correlated during recessions, while correlations between risk-on and "risk-off" assets (such as government bonds, which perform well during economic downturns) become more negative. In addition to these important cyclical variations, there are secular shifts in some key correlations that portfolio managers and asset owners need to understand. An example is the correlation between the returns on default-free bonds and equities. This correlation has switched from being mildly positive in the postwar period to being negative over the last 20 years. We examine the bond–equity correlation in detail to understand its historical drivers and present a model for assessing the outlook for this key relationship. We also characterize another important correlation for asset allocation: the correlation between credit spreads and equity returns. Allocations to equities and credit assets are two complementary ways of gaining exposure to risk-on assets. Hence, this correlation determines how diversified the procyclical part of a portfolio is.

3.1. Empirical Properties of the Volatility of Key Risk Factors

We begin our analysis of risk with an examination of risk factor volatilities in the postwar history. **Exhibit 3.1a** shows the annualized volatility of the risk factors based on monthly data for the full sample, over the last 20 years and over the last 6 years. The set of risk factors includes (1) excess returns (over the US dollar short rate) on a broad US equities index, (2) the excess returns (over duration-matched Treasuries) on a broad US investment-grade credit index, (3) a set of four US Treasury factors, and (4) excess returns (over the US dollar short rate) on two major currencies. The four Treasury factors are:

1. excess returns (over the short rate) on 2-year Treasuries,

2. returns on a long position in a 5-year forward contract on a 5-year Treasury security (this position benefits from a decline in the 5-year × 5-year Treasury yield and is a broad proxy for returns on Treasuries of intermediate maturities [5–10 years]),

3. excess returns (over the short rate) on 10-year Treasuries, and

4. returns on a 10-year versus 20-year steepener position (this is a position designed to profit when the differential between the 20-year Treasury yield and the 10-year Treasury yield—that is, the 10- to 20-year yield curve slope—increases).

Credit index excess returns and all US Treasury factors are measured *per unit of duration*. As a result, these factors also approximately equal the (*negative of*) changes in the credit spread of the index, changes in 2-year yields, changes in 5-year × 5-year yields, changes in 10-year yields, and changes in the 10- to 20-year yield curve slope. The details of factor measurement and data sources are given in the Appendix (item A.3.1).

Exhibit 3.1a.   Volatilities of Key Risk Factors in the United States (% per year)

	Return on a Broad Equity Index	Investment-Grade Credit Spread Return	2-Year Treasury Return	5-Year × 5-Year Treasury Return	10-Year Treasury Return	10-year to 20-Year Steepener Return	JPY	EUR
Full sample[a]	14.6	0.5	1.5	1.1	1.1	0.4	11.4	11.1
1995–2015	15.1	0.6	0.8	1.0	0.9	0.3	11.0	10.3
2010–2015	13.1	0.5	0.4	1.0	0.7	0.3	8.7	10.5

Notes: [a]The full sample period for credit spread returns is January 1973–December 2015, and for currencies, it is January 1975–December 2015. For all other variables, it is January 1955–December 2015. As of 31 December 2015. All returns are measured at a monthly frequency. For the broad equity index, we use the S&P 500 after January 1988. Prior to this date, we use returns on other proxies of the broad US equity market. Investment-grade credit spread return refers to the excess return over duration-matched Treasuries (per unit of duration) on the Barclays US Credit Index. This is a broad index of US investment-grade credit bonds. All Treasury yield curve factors are computed using constant-maturity US Treasury yields of various maturities as reported by the Federal Reserve; Gurkaynak, Sack, and Wright (2006); and Ibbotson Associates and returns on various Barclays US Treasury indices. For dates before the advent of the euro, returns on the German mark are used. The methodology for factor measurement and further details of data sources are given in the Appendix (items A.3.1 and A.3.2).

Sources: Barclays; Bloomberg; data library of Kenneth French; Federal Reserve; Gurkaynak, Sack, and Wright (2006); Haver Analytics; Ibbotson Associates; MSCI; PIMCO.

The long-sample and recent estimates reported in Exhibit 3.1a suggest that equity volatility of around 15% per year, volatility of Treasury yield changes of about 80–100 bps (that is, 0.8% to 1%) per year, volatility of credit spread changes of about 50–60 bps per year, and currency volatility of 10% per year are useful anchors to keep in mind. Also note that the gradual reduction in expected inflation and its volatility and the resulting stability in monetary policy contributed to a notable decline in the volatility of yield changes in the front end of the yield curve over the last 20 years. Additionally, the unusual monetary policy in the aftermath of the global financial crisis of 2008 led to further reduction in the volatility of interest rates (especially for short maturities), credit spreads, and equities.

The "term structure" of volatility estimates also exhibits interesting properties, as shown in **Exhibit 3.1b**. In the three decades prior to 1985, the volatility of short-maturity Treasuries sharply exceeded that of longer-dated ones. This property persisted till the advent of the policy of ultra-low interest rates. In the past five years, with monetary policy close to the "zero bound," the volatility of longer-maturity Treasuries has exceeded that of shorter-maturity

Exhibit 3.1b.   Volatilities of Treasury Returns (per Year of Duration) across the Term Structure (% per year)

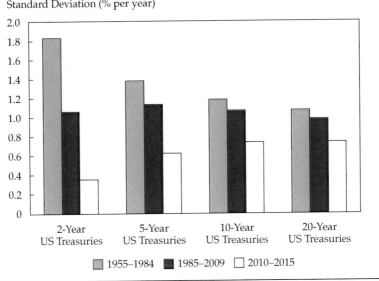

Note: As of 31 December 2015.
Sources: Barclays; Bloomberg; Federal Reserve; Gurkaynak, Sack, and Wright (2006); PIMCO.

ones. As we will show in Section 3.2, this pattern in the term structure of the volatility of yield changes is also reflected in the correlation between the returns to Treasuries and the returns to steepener positions.

Excess Volatility in Financial Markets. One of the most important features of financial markets is that they exhibit "excess volatility." As was pointed out by Shiller (1981) in his well-known critique, financial market volatility far exceeds most reasonable measures of the volatility of fundamentals. This effect is seen in **Exhibit 3.2.**

In Exhibit 3.2, we compare estimates of the volatility of equity returns (roughly 15% per year since 1955) with the volatilities of macro variables. The volatilities of real GDP and personal consumption expenditures (PCE) growth are modest at close to 2% per year. Corporate earnings, which constitute the claim of relatively junior stakeholders (i.e., the equity shareholders) on aggregate output, are more volatile, as expected, at 11% per year. Interestingly, the volatility of dividend growth is lower than that of earnings growth (at 6%–8% per year), reflecting dividend smoothing by corporations.

Equities ought to be priced as the present value of a stream of dividends. If discount rates were constant, one would get 6%–8% as the upper bound

Exhibit 3.2. Estimates of Volatility of Macro Variables vs. Equity Return Volatility, 1955–2015

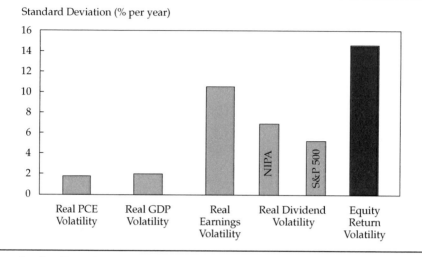

Standard Deviation (% per year)

Notes: As of 31 December 2015. For methodology and sources for equity returns, see Appendix (items A.3.1 and A.3.2). Returns data are at monthly frequency. Data for real earnings, GDP, and PCE (personal consumption expenditures) are from the US Bureau of Economic Analysis (BEA), obtained via Bloomberg. National income and product accounts (NIPA) dividends are from BEA and the Federal Reserve. S&P 500 dividends are from Robert Shiller's website.

Sources: Bloomberg; US Bureau of Economic Analysis; Federal Reserve; PIMCO; Robert Shiller's website (www.econ.yale.edu/~shiller).

of a fundamentally justifiable volatility level of equities. The fact that equity return volatility estimates are significantly higher than that level is consistent with the notion that a large part of the variation in equity returns is due to the time variation of risk premia. Furthermore, based on the bounds arrived at in Hansen and Jagannathan (1991), it can be shown that standard consumption-based asset-pricing models cannot explain the volatility of equity returns unless investors are assumed to be implausibly risk averse.

The significance of this excess volatility for investors is that it implies that risk premia might change frequently and sometimes excessively. Additionally, as we show in Chapter 5, valuations in asset markets tend to exhibit the property of slow mean reversion over medium horizons. Thus, the task of a macro-aware investment process is to judge when and where risk premia may have become extreme and position portfolios to take advantage of attractive valuations (and avoid unattractive ones).

Countercyclical Movements in Volatility. The fact that volatility in financial markets seems excessive relative to the volatility of fundamentals does not mean that market volatility shows no dependence on the macroeconomy. As **Exhibit 3.3** makes evident, a key consideration in a forward-looking assessment of risk is the macroeconomic outlook. Volatility is significantly higher in recessions than in expansions across the board. Over the past 60 years, equity return volatility has been 20% per year in recessions, compared with 13% per year in economic expansions. Credit markets are particularly sensitive to recessions. The volatility of changes in investment-grade credit spreads has been dramatically higher in recessions—close to 100–130 bps per year in recessions compared to 40 bps per year in expansions.

Exhibit 3.3. Volatilities of Key Risk Factors in the United States (% per year)

	Return on a Broad Equity Index	Investment-Grade Credit Spread Return	2-Year Treasury Return	5-Year × 5-Year Treasury Return	10-Year Treasury Return	10- to 20-Year Steepener Return	JPY	EUR
Full sample[a]	14.6	0.5	1.5	1.1	1.1	0.4	11.4	11.1
1995–2015	15.1	0.6	0.8	1.0	0.9	0.3	11.0	10.3
2010–2015	13.1	0.5	0.4	1.0	0.7	0.3	8.7	10.5
Full sample[a]								
Expansion	13.3	0.4	1.2	1.0	1.0	0.3	11.0	10.8
Recession	20.6	1.1	2.6	1.7	1.7	0.6	13.8	13.7
Since January 1986								
Expansion	14.1	0.4	0.9	1.0	1.0	0.3	11.2	10.5
Recession	22.4	1.4	1.1	1.6	1.2	0.3	12.2	14.7

Notes: [a]The full sample period for credit spread returns is January 1973–December 2015, and for currencies, it is January 1975–December 2015. For all other variables, it is January 1955–December 2015. As of 31 December 2015. All returns are measured at a monthly frequency. Recession dates are from the National Bureau of Economic Research (NBER). For factor definitions and sources, see notes to Exhibit 3.1a and items A.3.1 and A.3.2 in the Appendix.
Sources: Barclays; Bloomberg; data library of Kenneth French; Federal Reserve; Gurkaynak, Sack, and Wright (2006); Haver Analytics; Ibbotson Associates; MSCI; PIMCO.

Turning to interest rate factors, their volatility at first glance looks similarly sensitive to the business cycle. Over the full sample, the volatility during economic expansions has been 118 bps per year for the 2-year yields, 97 bps per year for the 10-year yields, and 31 bps per year for the long-end slope. The comparable volatilities in recessions were 254, 172, and 56 bps per year, respectively. However, most of these large differences are due to the extremely volatile inflation levels that the economy experienced in recessions during the 1970s and 1980s. In the more recent sample, since 1986, the volatility of Treasury yields has been much less variable across expansions and recessions—around 100 bps per year for 2-year and 10-year yields and 30 bps per year for the long-end slope.

To further illustrate the cyclical properties of volatility, we compare a composite score of US financial market volatility with the contemporaneous 24-month rolling average value of the Chicago Fed National Activity Index (CFNAI).[5] As is evident from **Exhibit 3.4**, these two series are negatively correlated. Note that the rolling average of CFNAI is plotted on an inverted scale in Exhibit 3.4. The correlation between the two series is −0.5. Thus, when the economy is expanding, financial market volatility is low; when the economy decelerates and falls into recession, volatility is relatively higher.

---

[5]The Chicago Fed National Activity Index is a monthly index designed to gauge broad economic activity in the United States and the associated inflationary pressure. It is computed as a weighted average of 85 monthly indicators of economic activity. The indicators are drawn from four broad categories of data: (1) production and income; (2) employment and hours worked; (3) personal consumption and housing; and (4) sales, orders, and inventories. Details can be found at https://www.chicagofed.org/publications/cfnai/index.

Exhibit 3.4. A Composite Score of US Financial Market Volatility and US Economic Activity, January 1977–December 2015

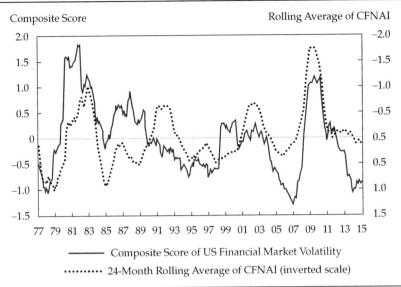

———— Composite Score of US Financial Market Volatility

·········· 24-Month Rolling Average of CFNAI (inverted scale)

Notes: As of 31 December 2015. The composite score of US financial market volatility is computed as follows: (1) First, we calculate the time series of 24-month rolling volatilities of all the risk factors that are shown in Exhibit 3.1a (except for the 5-year × 5-year Treasury returns); (2) next, we compute a corresponding time series of Z-scores for the volatility of each risk factor, where the Z-score for a given date equals the 24-month rolling volatility of the factor on that date less the full sample mean of the rolling volatility, divided by its full sample standard deviation; and (3) finally, we define the composite score of US financial market volatility at any date to be the cross-sectional average of the Z-scores of each risk factor's volatility on that date.

Sources: Bloomberg; Federal Reserve Bank of Chicago; PIMCO.

Level Dependence of Volatility in Fixed-Income Markets. This countercyclicality induces another feature of volatility that is of particular interest to fixed-income investors. The volatility of credit excess returns exhibits systematic covariation with the level of spreads. As a result, the volatility of changes in spreads of lower-rated bonds tends to be higher than that for higher-rated bonds, and spreads are more volatile during economic downturns and periods of financial stress.

Level dependence of credit spread volatility. **Exhibit 3.5a** shows a scatter plot of the volatility of monthly excess returns per unit of spread duration of various *sector × rating × maturity* buckets of a broad universe of US

Exhibit 3.5a. **Average Spread of US Corporate Bond Portfolios vs. Volatility of Excess Returns over Duration-Matched Treasuries, per Year of Spread Duration, January 1990–December 2015**

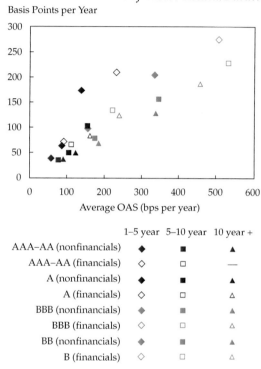

A. Standard Deviation of Excess Return/Duration

Basis Points per Year

	1–5 year	5–10 year	10 year +
AAA–AA (nonfinancials)	◆	■	▲
AAA–AA (financials)	◇	□	—
A (nonfinancials)	◆	■	▲
A (financials)	◇	□	△
BBB (nonfinancials)	◆	■	▲
BBB (financials)	◇	□	△
BB (nonfinancials)	◆	■	▲
B (financials)	◇	□	△

Notes: As of 31 December 2015. These computations use monthly data on excess returns (over duration-matched Treasuries) on various subdivisions of the Barclays US Corporate and Barclays US Corporate High Yield indices. See the Appendix to Chapter 2 (item A.2.2) for details.
Sources: Barclays POINT; PIMCO.

corporate bonds against the average spread levels of these buckets, both computed for the period January 1990–December 2015.[6]

In the cross section, the volatility of spread changes increases as the level of spreads increases. Indeed, as mentioned in Chapter 2, a more or less constant volatility model is obtained if we model the volatility of excess returns over Treasuries (per year of spread duration) of any portfolio of credit-risky bonds as being proportional to the starting level of spreads for that portfolio. This result is seen in **Exhibit 3.5b**, where we show a scatter plot of the

[6]This analysis uses the same data that is used for credit return regressions in Chapter 2. See the Appendix to Chapter 2 (item A.2.2) for details.

Exhibit 3.5b.   Average Spread of US Corporate Bond Portfolios vs. Volatility of Excess Returns over Duration-Matched Treasuries, per Year of Spread Duration *Times* Spread, January 1990–December 2015

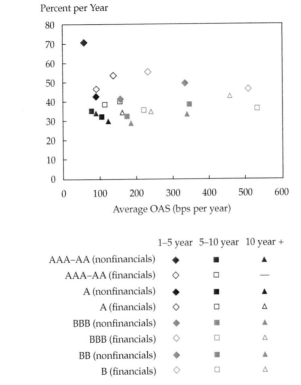

B. Standard Deviation of Excess Return/(Duration × Spread)

	1–5 year	5–10 year	10 year +
AAA–AA (nonfinancials)	◆	■	▲
AAA–AA (financials)	◇	□	—
A (nonfinancials)	◆	■	▲
A (financials)	◇	□	△
BBB (nonfinancials)	◆	■	▲
BBB (financials)	◇	□	△
BB (nonfinancials)	◆	■	▲
B (financials)	◇	□	△

Notes: As of 31 December 2015. These computations use monthly data on excess returns (over duration-matched Treasuries) on various subdivisions of the Barclays US Corporate and Barclays US Corporate High Yield indices. See the Appendix to Chapter 2 (item A.2.2) for details.
Sources: Barclays POINT; PIMCO.

estimates of the volatility of monthly excess returns (divided by spread duration *times* the level of spread at the start of the month) for various subindices in our sample.

This feature of spread movements has been well documented in previous research. See, for example, Ben Dor, Dynkin, Hyman, Houweling, van Leeuwen, and Penninga (2007), who argue that a good measure of the spread risk exposure of a credit-risky bond is its duration times spread.[7] Given this rather strong evidence for the link between spread levels and the near-term volatility of spread changes, we favor embedding this feature in the modeling of credit spread dynamics and in portfolio optimizations that include credit assets.

▨   *Level dependence of interest rate volatility.* This level dependence of volatility is, in fact, present in interest rates as well. To demonstrate this, we examine a range of specifications of the dynamics of Treasury yield volatility. We specify a model where the volatility of changes in Treasury yields of various maturities is of the form σy^γ, where y is the yield level, σ and γ are positive constants, and γ is between 0 and 1. If $\gamma = 0$, the volatility is constant (and equals σ). If $\gamma = 1$, then the volatility of yield changes is proportional to the yield level (for example, volatility would double if yields were to double). An intermediate behavior is obtained for, say, $\gamma = 0.5$. The constant γ measures the elasticity of the yield volatility with respect to changes in yield levels. (Hence, this model is known as the constant elasticity of variance [CEV] model.) The exact specification of our model is given in the Appendix (item A.3.3).

As a simple test of the degree of level dependence, we compute a time series of monthly yield changes normalized by their estimated beginning-of-month volatility (under the assumptions that $\gamma = 0$, 0.5, and 1). If a particular specification is good, then these *normalized* yield changes should have a standard deviation of 1.

In **Exhibit 3.6**, we present the standard deviations of normalized yield changes for $\gamma = 0$, 0.5, and 1, for yields of 2-, 5-, 10-, and 30-year maturities. The "$\gamma = 0$" model does a reasonably good job of forecasting volatility at the 10-year point: The standard deviation of normalized yield changes turns out to be close to 1. This model specification, however, does not perform well for maturities other than 10 years. In the case of 2-year Treasuries, for example, the standard deviation of normalized yield changes is close to 0.85. This means that this model, on average, *overestimated* volatility by roughly 15% over our sample. We end up normalizing by too large a volatility if we choose $\gamma = 0$. Most of this overestimation occurs in the past 10 years, which have

---

[7]If the volatility of spread changes were proportional to the spread of the bond, then a first-order approximation to the ith bond's excess return over and above duration-matched Treasuries from date t to $t + 1$ is $R(i,t,t + 1) \approx \alpha(t) + SD(i,t)S(t)\sigma(t)\delta(t + 1)$, where $R(i,t,t + 1)$ is the (excess) return on bond t from date t to $t + 1$, $\alpha(t)$ measures the expected excess return at date t, $SD(i,t)$ is the spread duration of the bond at date t, $S(t)$ is the spread that the bond is trading on at date t, $\sigma(t)$ is the volatility of proportional spread changes at date t, and $\delta(t + 1)$ is a zero-mean and unit variance random shock.

Exhibit 3.6. **Standard Deviation of (Normalized) Monthly Changes in Treasury Yields, by Model Specification, January 1990–December 2015**

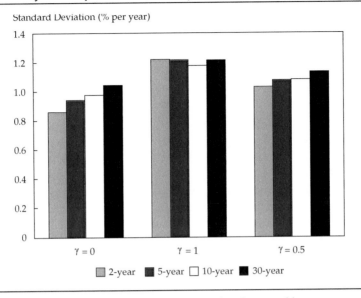

Notes: As of 31 December 2015. These computations are based on monthly excess returns over the short rate on Barclays US Treasury Bellwethers Index, *per unit of duration.* Excess returns through 2001 are computed relative to 1-month LIBOR less 5 bps, to adjust for the average credit spread embedded in LIBOR. From 2002 on, excess returns are computed over the 1-month overnight index swap (OIS) rate.
Sources: Barclays; Bloomberg; PIMCO.

been a period of extraordinarily low interest rate levels—and low volatility of rates at the front end of the yield curve due to monetary policy being stuck at the zero bound. Thus, there is a case for some level dependence of volatility.

However, the "$\gamma = 1$" model allows too much level dependence. Exhibit 3.6 shows that this model *underestimated* volatility by roughly 20% across maturities over the sample period. While interest rate volatility has fallen along with the level of rates, particularly in the front end of the yield curve, the decline in volatility has been less than that in the level of rates. Consequently, the "$\gamma = 1$" model does not quite work. However, an intermediate specification, with $\gamma = 0.5$, presents a good compromise and results in a decent overall fit. This finding indicates that some degree of level dependence is a good feature to incorporate into a model of interest rate volatility.

Mean Reversion of Volatility in Financial Markets. Given the relationship of volatility to the business cycle, as well as the dependence of volatility on yield levels and spreads in fixed-income markets, it should not be surprising that asset market volatility also exhibits the property of mean reversion. That is, when volatility has been higher or lower than average in the recent past, it tends to revert to a normal level over time. Considering, however, that the state of the macroeconomy tends to exhibit some persistence, we would expect that financial market volatility would mean-revert somewhat slowly. This behavior of volatility (i.e., its time variation, persistence, and stationarity) is consistent with the generalized autoregressive conditional heteroskedasticity (GARCH) process proposed by Engle (1982).

Exhibit 3.7 presents the time series of realized volatility of price returns of the S&P 500 (and its precessor indices) and of changes in 10-year US Treasury yields. We show estimates of trailing 1-month volatility and trailing 5-year volatility. Volatility is estimated using 3-day returns, sampled daily.[8]

While the longer-term volatility of returns on US equities has remained in the range of 12%–18% per year in the long sample and does not display a significant trend, the volatility of US Treasury yield changes has declined dramatically in the past three decades or so. Treasury yield volatility soared in

Exhibit 3.7. Realized Volatility of S&P 500 Returns and Changes in 10-Year US Treasury Yields (Trailing 1-Month vs. 5-Year Estimates), 1955–2015

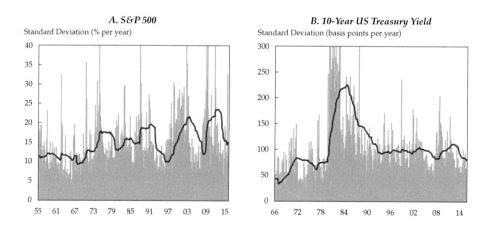

Notes: As of 31 December 2015. Trailing 1-month and 5-year rolling volatilities are computed using 3-day returns and 3-day yield changes, sampled daily. Data for 10-year US Treasury yields are from the Federal Reserve's Statistical Release H.15.
Sources: Bloomberg; Federal Reserve; PIMCO.

---

[8]We use 3-day price returns and 3-day yield changes to account for short-term reversals.

the period of high interest rates just before and during Paul Volcker's chairmanship of the Federal Reserve and has systematically declined since then. This decline can be loosely interpreted as an indication of the increase in the inflation-fighting credibility of the Federal Reserve—which has resulted in tighter anchoring of inflation expectations and consequently lower volatility of long rates. One could therefore argue that this persistent decline in interest rate volatility over the past three decades is unlikely to repeat. This evidence also demonstrates the need to account for the effect of such one-off factors in estimating the dynamics of financial market volatility over shorter horizons.

It is also possible to get a sense of the speed of mean reversion in volatility. To this end, we estimate the following model for the dynamics of volatility in interest rate and equity markets:

$$\begin{pmatrix} \text{1-month volatility} \\ -\text{Trailing 5-year volatility} \end{pmatrix} = \alpha + \beta \text{ lagged} \begin{pmatrix} \text{1-month volatility} \\ -\text{Trailing 5-year volatility} \end{pmatrix} + \varepsilon.$$

We can think of the 5-year trailing volatility as an estimate of the long-term volatility of the underlying returns and postulate that large deviations of recently realized volatility from this long-term estimate will tend to normalize over time. The parameter β measures the speed of mean reversion. For example, if $\beta = 0.75$ when the lag is one month, then 25% of the deviation between 1-month trailing volatility and 5-year trailing volatility is expected to reverse over a 1-month horizon. The exact specification of our model is given in the Appendix (item A.3.4).

In **Exhibit 3.8**, the grey bars represent estimates of β for lags of 1, 3, 6, and 12 months, estimated using the volatility of S&P 500 returns over the past 60 years and in the post-Volcker period. We show that over the 1955–2015 period, roughly 40% of the deviation of short-term (1-month horizon) volatility estimates from longer-term (5-year horizon) volatility reversed over a 1-month horizon—leaving 60% of the gap on average at the end of one month. Thus, a nontrivial proportion of deviations in volatility reverse over a short horizon. If the reversal of the deviation were to continue at the same pace, roughly 25% of it would remain at the end of 3 months, 6% at 6 months, and none at 12 months. These estimates are presented on the red line, labeled "AR(1)." The fact that the grey bars lie well above the red line indicates that equity volatility has also exhibited persistence over the medium term. Results are similar in the post-Volcker period.

Exhibit 3.8. Estimates of Persistence (β) for Volatility of Returns on the S&P 500, 1955–2015 vs. 1987–2015

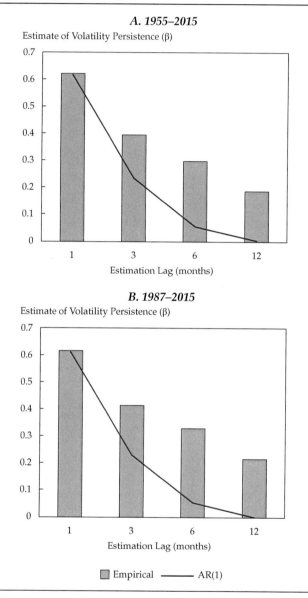

A. 1955–2015

Estimate of Volatility Persistence (β)

Estimation Lag (months)

B. 1987–2015

Estimate of Volatility Persistence (β)

Estimation Lag (months)

▢ Empirical ──── AR(1)

Notes: As of 31 December 2015. These computations use monthly data on trailing 1-month and 5-year volatilities of price returns on the S&P 500. Trailing 1-month and 5-year volatilities are computed using 3-day returns, sampled daily. See Appendix (item A.3.4) for details of the regression specification.

Sources: Bloomberg; PIMCO.

In **Exhibit 3.9**, we present estimates of β for lags of 1, 3, 5, and 12 months for the volatility of changes in 10-year US Treasury yields. In the sample since 1966, we find that roughly 40% of deviations reverse over a month, which is similar to the finding for equities (Exhibit 3.8). However, we find that roughly 40% of deviations remain even at the end of 12 months, which indicates a much greater degree of persistence in interest rate markets than in equity markets. However, as pointed out in Exhibit 3.7, this result is driven in large part by the persistent increase in volatility leading up to the late 1970s and the systematic decline in volatility since then. When we focus on the post-1987 period, we find that the speed of reversion of deviations in volatility (vs. long-term estimates) is a lot higher. Over a month, roughly 55% of the deviation reverses, and over 12 months, roughly 80% reverses—a result that is roughly in line with what we documented in the case of S&P 500 volatility.

This evidence of short-run reversal and medium-term persistence in volatility has important implications for the measurement and forecasting of portfolio risk. The best practice is to combine long-term estimates of volatility with estimates that overweight recent observations, rather than relying solely on either. With this approach, one is less likely to be lulled into serenity following periods that have been less volatile, nor is one likely to de-risk portfolios excessively following periods of heightened volatility.

Exhibit 3.9.   Estimates of Persistence (β) for Volatility of Changes in 10-Year US Treasury Yields, 1966–2015 vs. 1987–2015

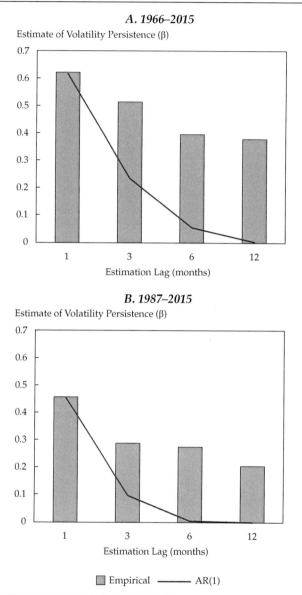

A. 1966–2015

Estimate of Volatility Persistence (β)

B. 1987–2015

Estimate of Volatility Persistence (β)

Estimation Lag (months)

☐ Empirical ——— AR(1)

Notes: As of 31 December 2015. These computations use monthly data on trailing 1-month and 5-year volatilities of changes in 10-year US Treasury yields. Trailing 1-month and 5-year volatilities are computed using 3-day yield changes, sampled daily. See Appendix (item A.3.4) for details of the regression specification.

Sources: Bloomberg; PIMCO.

3.2. Correlation of Risk Factors

The second essential element in measuring the risk of a portfolio is the matrix of correlations between risk factors. Financial market practitioners find it useful to classify risk factors into those that tend to react favorably to positive shocks to growth and risk appetite ("risk-on" factors) and those that react positively when the news about the economy is negative and risk aversion is rising ("risk-off" factors). The correlation of various risk factors with equities is often used to classify them into these categories. The correlation matrices reported below are helpful in understanding the risk-on versus risk-off nature of various risk factors.

Exhibit 3.10 shows pairwise correlations over the full sample from 1955, as well as over the last 20 years, for returns to a selection of key risk factors.

As expected, the risk factor that is most highly correlated with equities is the credit spread component of default-risky bonds. This factor has a full sample equity correlation of 0.36. This correlation has increased to 0.55 over the last 20 years (since 1995), when real business cycle fluctuations, not fluctuations in inflation, have been the main source of macroeconomic volatility. Credit spreads have consistently tended to widen when equities have sold off.

Over the full sample, Treasury returns and equity returns have been modestly positively correlated. Importantly, however, over the last 20 years, this correlation has shifted to a markedly negative correlation of about −0.2 (for both short-term and intermediate rates). Hence, more recently, we see that duration exposure tends to effectively diversify risk-on assets, which perform well when equities perform poorly. The curve steepener (a long position in 10-year Treasuries and a short position in 20-year Treasuries) also behaves as a mildly risk-off asset; that is, the curve tends to steepen during sell-offs in equity and credit markets. In Section 3.3, we examine the change in the bond–equity correlation in greater detail and find that this change partly reflects a shift in macroeconomic risk from inflation, which was the dominant risk in the 1970s and early 1980s, to volatility in real growth from 1990 to the present day, a period when inflation expectations have been fairly stable.

The EUR/USD exchange rate[9] is modestly positively correlated with equities, with realized correlations of 0.1 and 0.2 over the full sample and over the last 20 years, respectively. Thus, the US dollar tends to strengthen against the euro (and, in fact, against most currencies) in crisis episodes when US assets are perceived as a "safe haven." Such a scenario increases demand for liquid US assets, such as Treasuries, and puts upward pressure on the US

---

[9]Before the introduction of the euro in 1999, we use returns to a long 1-month forward in German marks (DEM/USD).

Exhibit 3.10. Pairwise Correlations of Key US Risk Factors

	Full Sample*						1995–2015					
	Investment Grade Credit Spread Return	2-Year Treasury Return	5-Year x 5-Year Treasury Return	10-Year –20-Year Steepener Return	JPY	EUR	Investment Grade Credit Spread Return	2-Year Treasury Return	5-Year x 5-Year Treasury Return	10- to 20-Year Steepener Return	JPY	EUR
Return on a Broad Equity Index	0.36	0.11	0.15	-0.05	-0.04	0.08	0.55	-0.27	-0.15	-0.10	-0.04	0.19
Return on a Broad Equity Index		-0.17	-0.26	-0.08	-0.10	0.07		-0.37	-0.21	-0.16	-0.16	0.23
2-Year Treasury Return			0.60	0.44	0.22	0.22			0.56	0.64	0.32	0.17
5-Year x 5-Year Treasury Return				0.15	0.11	0.09				0.18	0.18	0.10
10- to 20-Year Steepener Return					0.16	0.12					0.27	0.26
JPY						0.46						0.24

Notes: As of 31 December 2015. The correlations presented here are for the risk factors considered in Exhibits 3.1a and 3.3. Data frequency is monthly. *Full sample correlations for US investment-grade credit spread returns are from January 1973, while full sample correlations for EUR/USD and JPY/USD are from January 1975. Otherwise, correlations are from February 1955. For factor definitions and data sources, see notes to Exhibit 3.1a and the Appendix (items A.3.1 and A.3.2).

Sources: NBER; PIMCO.

dollar. The positive correlation with equities would also be a feature of the returns of emerging market currencies versus the US dollar, considering that the demand for emerging market assets wanes markedly in periods of stress. The Japanese yen is a notable exception in this respect, behaving as a risk-off asset versus equities and credit.

As with risk factor volatilities, the macroeconomic outlook plays a key role in determining the correlations between risk factors. As **Exhibit 3.11** illustrates, correlations typically become more extreme in recessions, especially when we look at the more recent period, since 1986. Importantly, credit–equity correlations "jump" from 0.37 in expansions to 0.58 in recessions. We examine the resulting nonlinearity of credit's beta to equity in Section 3.4. The hedging properties of risk-off assets also tend to become exaggerated in recessions; for example, the correlation of the Japanese yen with US equities goes from −0.04 in expansions to −0.24 in recessions, while the realized correlation of the front end of the yield curve with US equities drops from 0 to −0.34 in recessions. Likewise, the correlation of the long-end steepener with US equities declines substantially, from 0.01 to −0.37, due to cyclical variation in policy rates set by central banks.

The effect of macroeconomic factors on correlations can also be detected in a comparison of the correlation matrix for the long sample with that for the post–financial crisis period, as shown in **Exhibit 3.12a**. The steepener became positively correlated with risk-on assets in the 2010–2015 period. This result is due to the fact that the slope of the curve was driven solely by long rates, as short-term rates were expected to remain pinned at zero for an extended period of time. As mentioned earlier, the term structure of yield volatilities over this period also reflects this observation, since a positive correlation between long-dated yields and the slope of the curve leads to the volatility of yield changes being higher at the long end than at intermediate maturities.

The positive correlation between long yields and equity returns was then reflected in the correlation of the curve slope with equities. We can also see a much larger correlation between currencies and equities in this period. The correlation between EUR/USD and equities increases from 0.19 in the 1995–2015 period to 0.56 in the past five years. This finding potentially reflects the effect of the sovereign debt crisis period in the euro area, when the euro and equities (particularly European equities) both underperformed. In fact, after the European Central Bank decisively started its program of sovereign bond buying (Outright Monetary Transactions, or OMT) in 2012, this correlation gradually reversed sign, as seen in **Exhibit 3.12b**. With massive quantitative easing in progress, equity rallies were associated with currency weakness.

Exhibit 3.11. Correlations of Key US Risk Factors in Expansions and in Recessions

Expansions (Full Sample)

	Investment Grade Credit Spread Return	2-Year Treasury Return	5-Year x 5-Year Treasury Return	10- to 20-Year Steepener Return	JPY	EUR
Return on a Broad Equity Index	0.29	0.12	0.08	0.06	-0.03	0.04
Investment Grade Credit Spread Return		-0.24	-0.42	-0.05	-0.15	0.01
2-Year Treasury Return			0.55	0.48	0.17	0.22
5-Year x 5-Year Treasury Return				0.23	0.11	0.03
10- to 20-Year Steepener Return					0.12	0.22
JPY						0.47

Recessions (Full Sample)

	Investment Grade Credit Spread Return	2-Year Treasury Return	5-Year x 5-Year Treasury Return	10- to 20-Year Steepener Return	JPY	EUR
Return on a Broad Equity Index	0.55	0.21	0.30	-0.17	-0.04	0.30
Investment Grade Credit Spread Return		-0.02	0.02	-0.12	-0.01	0.23
2-Year Treasury Return			0.62	0.37	0.37	0.31
5-Year x 5-Year Treasury Return				0.18	0.12	0.30
10- to 20-Year Steepener Return					0.29	-0.15
JPY						0.37

(continued)

Exhibit 3.11. Correlations of Key US Risk Factors in Expansions and in Recessions (continued)

Expansions (since 1986)

	Investment Grade Credit Spread Return	2-Year Treasury Return	5-Year x 5-Year Treasury Return	10- to 20-Year Steepener Return	JPY	EUR
Return on a Broad Equity Index	0.37	0.00	-0.01	0.01	-0.04	0.03
Investment Grade Credit Spread Return		-0.37	-0.47	-0.07	-0.17	0.06
2-Year Treasury Return			0.61	0.57	0.22	0.23
5-Year x 5-Year Treasury Return				0.15	0.15	0.00
10- to 20-Year Steepener Return					0.18	0.30
JPY						0.46

Recessions (since 1986)

	Investment Grade Credit Spread Return	2-Year Treasury Return	5-Year x 5-Year Treasury Return	10- to 20-Year Steepener Return	JPY	EUR
Return on a Broad Equity Index	0.58	-0.34	0.17	-0.37	-0.24	0.28
Investment Grade Credit Spread Return		-0.50	-0.05	-0.29	-0.18	0.24
2-Year Treasury Return			0.42	0.61	0.38	0.12
5-Year x 5-Year Treasury Return				-0.09	-0.01	0.46
10- to 20-Year Steepener Return					0.27	-0.07
JPY						0.25

Notes: As of 31 December 2015. The correlations presented here are for the risk factors considered in Exhibits 3.1 and 3.3. Data frequency is monthly. Full sample correlations for US investment-grade credit spread returns use data from January 1973, while full sample correlations for EUR/USD and JPY/USD use data from January 1975. Otherwise, correlations use data from February 1955. For factor definitions and data sources, see notes to Exhibit 3.1a and the Appendix (items A.3.1 and A.3.2). Recession dates are from NBER.

Sources: NBER; PIMCO.

Exhibit 3.12a. Correlations of Key US Risk Factors in the Long Sample and in the Post–Financial Crisis Period, January 1995–December 2015

1995–2015

	Investment Grade Credit Spread Return	2-Year Treasury Return	5-Year x 5-Year Treasury Return	10- to 20-year Steepener Return	JPY	EUR
Return on a Broad Equity Index	0.55	−0.27	−0.15	−0.10	−0.04	0.17
Investment Grade Credit Spread Return		−0.37	−0.21	−0.16	−0.16	0.23
2-Year Treasury Return			0.56	0.64	0.32	0.17
5-Year x 5-Year Treasury Return				0.18	0.18	0.10
10- to 20-Year Steepener Return					0.27	0.26
JPY						0.24

2010–2015

	Investment Grade Credit Spread Return	2-Year Treasury Return	5-Year x 5-Year Treasury Return	10- to 20-Year Steepener Return	JPY	EUR
Return on a Broad Equity Index	0.74	−0.25	−0.57	0.24	−0.31	0.56
Investment Grade Credit Spread Return		−0.21	0.52	0.22	−0.18	0.50
2-Year Treasury Return			0.51	0.53	0.47	−0.07
5-Year x 5-Year Treasury Return				−0.03	0.35	−0.48
10- to 20-Year Steepener Return					0.17	0.34
JPY						0.02

Notes: As of 31 December 2015. The correlations presented here are for the risk factors considered in Exhibits 3.1 and 3.3. Data frequency is monthly. For factor definitions and data sources, see the notes to Exhibit 3.1a and the Appendix (items A.3.1 and A.3.2).
Sources: NBER; PIMCO.

Exhibit 3.12b. **Rolling 13-Week and 52-Week Correlations between % Changes in EUR/USD Exchange Rate and EURO STOXX 50 Price Returns, January 2013–December 2015**

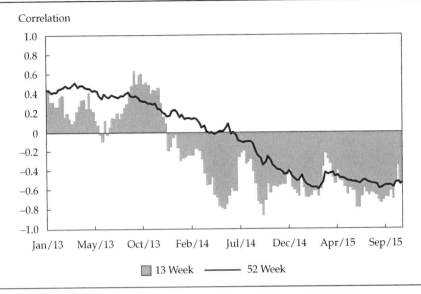

Notes: As of 31 December 2015. The 20-year monthly correlation equals −0.01%.
Sources: Bloomberg; PIMCO.

3.3. The Correlation between Default-Free Bonds and Equities

Investments in bonds play a pivotal role in multi-asset portfolios, both because short-horizon returns of bonds (i.e., returns over monthly or quarterly periods) tend to be negatively correlated with those of equities and because bonds tend to outperform in periods of economic weakness, when equities underperform. For these reasons, the correlation between stocks and bonds is arguably the most important correlation input to the asset allocation decision. Below, we look at some empirical properties of this correlation.

Exhibit 3.13a shows the history of the correlation between the excess returns (over the short rate) on a broad index of US equities and those on long-dated (20-year) Treasuries from June 1927 to June 2015. The bond–equity correlation has changed substantially over time and has responded to secular as well as cyclical changes in macroeconomic conditions.

The full sample average of the realized correlation is 10%, but there has been substantial variation around this mean. The range of the rolling 12-month correlation is remarkably wide, with a minimum of −93%, a

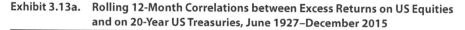

Exhibit 3.13a.   Rolling 12-Month Correlations between Excess Returns on US Equities and on 20-Year US Treasuries, June 1927–December 2015

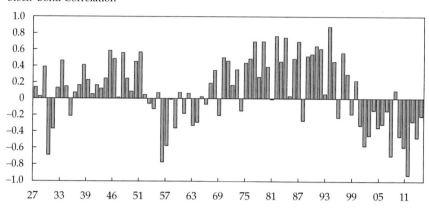

Notes: As of 31 December 2015. US equity returns are monthly and taken to be those of the market factor from the data library of Kenneth French until December 1954. After this date, the equity returns are as described in the Appendix (items A.3.1 and A.3.2). Returns to 20-year Treasuries use data from Ibbotson Associates for returns and yields on long-term (20-year) US Treasury bonds until 1981. From 1982 on, Treasury returns are as described in the Appendix (items A.3.1 and A.3.2). For the period 1927–1954, excess returns are over returns to 3-month Treasury bills. From 1955 on, excess returns are computed as described in the Appendix (items A.3.1 and A.3.2).
Sources: Barclays; data library of Kenneth French; Ibbotson Associates; PIMCO.

---

maximum of +86%, and a standard deviation of 40%. This correlation was below –50% in seven years and above +50% in 14 years. Persistently positive correlations in the 1970s and 1980s gave way to persistently negative values starting in the late 1990s. Negative correlations were also observed during the 1950s and during the Great Depression. Nonetheless, the persistence of the recent "regime," with a negative correlation between bond returns and equity returns, stands out as exceptional in the long historical time series.

The opposite sensitivities of government bonds and equities to cyclical downturns are what push the correlation between them to be negative. As seen in **Exhibit 3.13b**, five out of the nine recessions in the US economy in the last 60 years witnessed underperformance of equities and outperformance of 10-year US Treasuries (seven out of nine recessions in the case of 2-year US Treasuries). The recessions in which both assets underperformed were characterized by large inflation shocks (and by the extraordinary monetary policy response to such shocks during the twin recessions of 1979–1982).

Exhibit 3.13b.   Performance of Equities and Treasuries in US NBER Recessions, January 1955–December 2015

Start (3 months prior to recession)	End (halfway through recession)	US Equities	US Treasury 2-Year	US Treasury 10-Year
Returns in units of full sample volatility				
Jun 57	Jan 58	−1.5	0.5	0.5
Feb 60	Oct 60	−0.3	1.6	1.1
Oct 69	Jun 70	−1.7	0.0	−0.5
Sep 73	Aug 74	−2.5	−2.0	−1.2
Nov 79	May 80	−0.1	0.5	−0.1
May 81	Apr 82	−1.8	−0.4	−0.1
May 90	Dec 90	−0.3	1.2	1.0
Jan 01	Aug 01	−0.9	1.2	0.3
Oct 07	Oct 08	−1.8	1.3	1.0
Equally weighted average		−1.2	0.4	0.2
Pooled		−1.5	0.4	0.2
Pooled, excluding 1973–1982		−1.3	1.2	0.7
Full sample volatility (%)		14.6	1.5	1.1

Notes: As of 31 December 2015. Recession dates are from NBER. Factor definitions are described in the Appendix (items A.3.1 and A.3.2).
Source: NBER.

A Macro Factor Model for the Stock–Bond Correlation. One important question for investors is whether the correlation is going to stay negative in the future, providing strong diversification benefits between bonds and equities, or whether this correlation will become less negative or perhaps positive going forward.

To answer this question, we use an econometric model that relates the stock–bond correlation to the volatilities and correlations of three key macroeconomic factors: inflation, unemployment, and growth. Our model enables us to estimate correlations for various investment horizons. Thus, we can account for the fact that short-term and longer-run correlations may differ. In the short run, stocks and bonds tend to respond in opposite directions to fluctuations in investor risk appetite. During flight-to-safety episodes, when the expected risk premium on risky assets increases, we typically observe a negative correlation. However, at longer frequencies, shorter-term fluctuations in risk premia may be less important and the correlation can be dominated by more persistent shocks to inflation, which could result in a more positive correlation. The details of our econometric model are presented in the Appendix (item B.3.1).

Exhibit 3.14 presents an example of how our model can be used to project the stock–bond correlation over various horizons.

The short-run correlation is negative and close to −0.3 because the "flight to quality" effect dominates the effects of interest rates and inflation. However, as the investment horizon increases, the correlation becomes less negative because shocks to inflation drive bond yields and earnings yields in the same direction (higher inflation means higher yields and lower asset prices), and these shocks are relatively persistent. Inflation shocks therefore play a relatively larger role in shaping the long-run dynamics of earnings yields and bond yields and in determining the magnitude of the longer-run correlation, and they tend to exert less influence in the short term.

A sensitivity analysis of the impact of inflation volatility and real business cycle volatility (growth and unemployment) on our model-implied correlations is shown in **Exhibit 3.15**. Correlations become more positive (for all horizons) if we assume twice the amount of inflation volatility, holding all other factors constant. Higher inflation volatility could be interpreted as reflecting weaker inflation-fighting credentials of the central bank. As was seen in the late 1970s in the United States, weaker central bank credibility can go along with more positive correlation between bonds and equities. If

Exhibit 3.14. Term Structure of Stock–Bond Correlation Projections

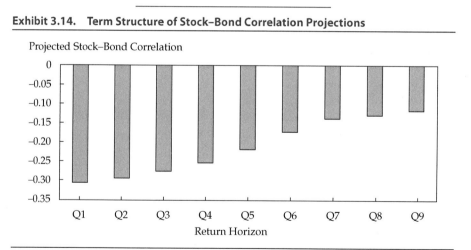

Notes: Hypothetical example, for illustration only. Simulations based on parameter estimates as of Q3 2013.
Source: PIMCO.

Exhibit 3.15. Term Structure of Correlations: Sensitivity to Inflation Volatility

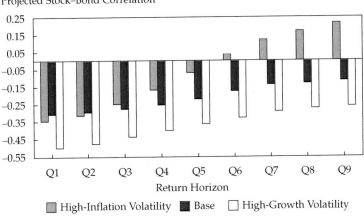

Projected Stock–Bond Correlation

Notes: Hypothetical example, for illustration only. Simulations based on parameter estimates as of Q3 2013.
Source: PIMCO.

we instead assume twice the amount of real business cycle volatility (higher growth and unemployment volatility), the correlation becomes more negative.

This analysis reveals that, while we continue to see a negative correlation as our base case, model-implied correlations are sensitive to changes in the macro environment. If inflation volatility does not change significantly, the correlation should remain negative, even at the 2-year horizon. On the other hand, if inflation volatility increases, our model clearly shows some "tail risk" in the hedging effect of bonds on equity risk. If inflation volatility increases significantly, the stock–bond correlation rises to +20% for 2-year returns. Bonds would still provide diversification benefits to risk assets, but perhaps not as much as investors are currently assuming in their asset allocation decisions. Thus, the outlook for macroeconomic risk is a critical consideration in evaluating the attractiveness of duration as a hedge for equity and credit spread exposures.

The above reasoning is motivated by the parameter estimates of our model (reported in the Appendix to this chapter). These estimates are informed by the experience of the last 30 years, when positive shocks to inflation expectations caused both equities and Treasuries to underperform in anticipation of a hawkish monetary policy response. It is worth thinking about whether this behavior will continue to hold if a hyperinflationary environment occurs, caused perhaps by monetization of public debt in highly indebted economies facing low (or negative) growth. One can argue that equities are real assets whose value should not erode in such environments while nominal securities might lose most of their value. In such extreme conditions, then, one might again see a negative correlation between stocks and bonds.

3.4.   The Covariation between Equities and Credit Spreads

The covariation between equities and credit spreads is a crucial input to managing the risk of multi-asset-class portfolios. If credit appears cheap relative to equities, for example, portfolio managers may choose to take equity risk via credit-risky bonds—and in such cases, it is important to have a good *ex ante* estimate of the risk of these positions.

As we show in **Exhibit 3.16**, the beta of investment-grade credit spread returns to equity returns has varied significantly over time. In this exhibit, we plot the level of the credit spread of the Barclays US Corporate Index and the rolling 36-month beta of excess returns of this index (over Treasuries, scaled to one year of spread duration) to the excess returns of the S&P 500 over cash. The sensitivity of credit spreads to equities rises significantly in periods of stress: Note that it doubled between the beginning and end of 2008.

Exhibit 3.16.   Level of Credit Spreads and Rolling 36-Month Beta of Excess Returns on US Corporate Index to Returns on S&P 500, January 1999– December 2015

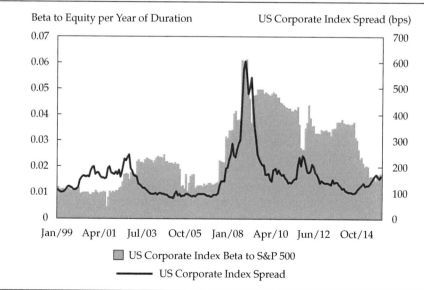

Notes: As of 31 December 2015. Regression betas are computed using monthly data.
Sources: Barclays; Bloomberg; PIMCO.

The dramatic increase in the beta of credit spreads to equities is expected, based on the dependence of credit excess return volatility on the level of credit spreads. In periods of stress, spread levels widen, leading to an increase in the volatility and equity beta of credit excess returns. The increase in the equity sensitivity of credit can also be justified theoretically. Merton's (1974) valuation model for the capital structure of the firm posits that equity should behave like a call option on the assets of the firm, whereas risky debt should behave like a riskless bond plus a short position in a put option on the firm's assets. The short option position embedded in credit-risky bonds leads to negative convexity in their payoff profile (e.g., for a zero-coupon risky bond, the best payoff is return of principal, but on the downside, the entire principal could be lost). As a result, the relationship between credit and equity returns becomes stronger in the Merton model when firm and equity valuations fall.

The key implication of this phenomenon is that credit risk exposure represents a nonlinear exposure to the value of the firm. As long as the firm is well capitalized and the leverage applied to the firm's equity is low, there is an equity cushion that protects debtholders from default and loss of principal. The put option embedded in risky debt is far out of the money, and default risk is consequently very low. In such environments, then, the linkages between marginal changes in equity valuations and credit valuations are weak. However, if a macroeconomic shock causes corporate earnings to fall and free cash flows consequently decline, earnings uncertainty increases and the equity cushion is reduced. The equity put option position gets closer to the money, and the relationship between credit and equity tightens.[10]

The phenomenon of higher equity sensitivity observed in time series (in Exhibit 3.16) is also seen in the cross section of credit sectors. In the first panel of **Exhibit 3.17**, we present estimates of the beta of excess returns of the credit index by rating bucket (all scaled to one year of spread duration at the beginning of each month) to the returns of the S&P 500. We use subindices of the Barclays US Corporate Index and the Barclays US Corporate High Yield Index for these calculations. These estimates imply, for example, that a 100 bp drop in the S&P 500 Index is associated with 2 bps (2% × 100 bps) of negative excess return (per year of duration) for Aa rated bonds. But for B rated bonds, the negative excess return (per year of duration) is 10.9 bps. As expected, the equity sensitivity of credit rises as ratings deteriorate. Also, the R^2 of the regressions rises as ratings decline, from approximately 20% for Aa rated credit to roughly 40% for B and Caa rated credit. This result is in line

---

[10]A similar prediction is made by Davydov and Linetsky (2001) and Carr and Linetsky (2006), who directly model the link between the firm's equity and debt.

Exhibit 3.17. Credit Spread Sensitivities (Betas) to Equity Market, by Rating and Maturity Bucket, January 1999–December 2015

	Aa	A	Baa	Ba	B	Caa	Investment Grade 1–3 Years	Investment Grade 3–5 Years
per year of duration								
Beta	2.0%	2.7%	3.5%	7.7%	10.9%	17.1%	3.4%	3.2%
R^2	22%	27%	32%	39%	41%	40%	17%	26%
per unit of duration × trailing average credit spread								
Beta	1.5%	1.5%	1.4%	1.8%	1.8%	1.6%	1.9%	1.7%
R^2	26%	30%	36%	39%	41%	42%	20%	29%

Notes: As of December 2015. Regression betas are computed using monthly excess returns on the S&P 500 and monthly excess returns and credit spreads of subdivisions of the Barclays US Corporate Index and the Barclays US Corporate High Yield Index.
Sources: Barclays; Bloomberg; PIMCO.

with the notion that for lower-quality credit, the option to default is closer to being in the money—leading to a tighter relationship with equity.

The evidence in Exhibits 3.5a and 3.5b suggests that we should account for the level of spreads in estimating the equity sensitivity of credit. To do so, we run regressions of credit excess returns of different rating and maturity buckets (adjusting for both duration and spread levels) on the excess returns of equities, as follows:

$$\frac{\text{Excess return}\left(i^{th}\text{ bucket}\right)}{\text{Spread duration }(i) \times \text{ Average spread}(i)} = \alpha(i)$$

$$+ \beta(i)\text{ Excess return}\left(\text{equity market index}\right)+ \varepsilon.$$

See the Appendix (item A.3.5) for a full description.

The results of this regression are presented in the lower panel of Exhibit 3.17. As expected, adjusting for the level of spreads significantly reduces the variation in equity sensitivity across rating buckets. Interestingly, however, this adjustment does not improve the power of equities to explain the variation of credit excess returns. The R^2 of the regression using spread-adjusted returns as the dependent variable is similar to those of the regressions without spread adjustments.

Equity Sensitivity of Credit in Down Markets. The negatively convex payoff profile of risky debt has the additional implication that the sensitivity to equities is larger on the downside than it is on the upside. This effect also contributes to the time-series variations in equity beta observed in Exhibit 3.16. In order to quantify this effect, we extend the above regression to estimate the equity beta of (normalized) excess returns of various rating buckets in up and down markets separately. A full description of our specification is given in the Appendix (item A.3.6).

We present the results of this regression in **Exhibit 3.18**. We find, consistently, that even after adjusting for duration and spread levels, the spread sensitivity of credit excess returns tends to be larger in down markets than in up markets. We also show that short-maturity credit spreads tend to exhibit greater downside sensitivity to equities than the broad credit universe. This pattern is in line with the fact that the return distribution of credit exhibits negative skewness, particularly in highly rated and low-duration credit buckets.

Exhibit 3.18. Credit Spread Sensitivities (Betas) to Equity Market in Up and Down Markets, by Rating and Maturity Bucket, January 1999–December 2015

	Aa	A	Baa	Ba	B	Caa	Investment Grade 1–3 Years	Investment Grade 3–5 Years
Up beta	0.9%	0.9%	0.7%	1.0%	0.8%	1.2%	1.1%	0.9%
Down beta	1.5%	1.6%	1.7%	1.9%	1.9%	1.7%	2.3%	2.0%
R^2	27%	31%	38%	41%	44%	43%	21%	30%

Notes: As of December 2015. Regression betas are computed using monthly excess returns on the S&P 500 and monthly excess returns and credit spreads of subdivisions of the Barclays US Corporate Index and the Barclays US Corporate High Yield Index.
Sources: PIMCO; Bloomberg; Barclays.

These observations matter in the context of portfolio construction because indirect equity beta exposures can be substantial. **Exhibit 3.19** shows the example of a hypothetical credit portfolio that is invested in both investment-grade and high-yield bonds across the term structure of spreads. The bulk of its exposure is concentrated in Baa rated credit (55% of market value), which contributes 0.04 of equity beta in up markets. The equity beta of this exposure more than doubles in down markets, contributing 0.09 in such periods. The contribution of front-end exposures, while small in absolute terms, tends

Exhibit 3.19. Indirect Equity Exposures of a Hypothetical Credit Portfolio: Example

	Allocation	Duration	Credit Spread (average)	Up Beta per Duration x Spread	Down Beta per Duration x Spread	Up Beta	Down Beta
Investment grade 1–3 years	15%	2 years	100 bps	1.1%	2.3%	0.00	0.01
Baa 5-year	55%	5 years	200 bps	0.7%	1.7%	0.04	0.09
Ba 5-year	30%	5 years	400 bps	1.0%	1.9%	0.06	0.11
Portfolio	**100%**	**4.6 years**	**245 bps**			**0.10**	**0.22**

Notes: As of 31 December 2015. Hypothetical example, for illustration only.

also to increase in down markets. Overall, the indirect equity exposure of this hypothetical portfolio adds up to 0.10 in up markets and increases materially, to 0.22, in down markets. Of course, a credit portfolio with a higher percentage allocation to high-yield credit would have a significantly higher equity beta and a much larger increase in equity beta in down markets.

3.5. Lessons for Asset Allocation

Properly assessing the risk portion of the risk–reward trade-off requires a nuanced view of the historical record and the underlying macroeconomic drivers of factor returns. The properties of risk factor volatilities—such as their countercyclicality, their level dependence, their mean reversion over short horizons, and their persistence over the medium term—are robustly present in the data. An asset allocation exercise must account for these properties. For example, a macro-aware asset allocator should assess the likelihood of an economic expansion continuing versus the economy falling into a contraction before deciding on the appropriate volatility parameters. Similarly, the level dependence of credit spread volatility implies that measurement of the exposure of a portfolio to credit spread changes should be sensitive to the current level of spreads.

Correlations that are critical for portfolio construction, such as the stock–bond correlation, have varied substantially over time. The relative importance of real growth risk and inflation risk are key determinants of the stock-bond correlation. The more predominant the real growth risk, the more negative the stock–bond correlation, while the greater relative importance of inflation risk induces a more positive correlation. If our forecast is of relatively contained inflation risk, we should see the negative correlation between stocks and bonds persisting. However, the potential for elevated inflation risk and the risk of a higher stock–bond correlation should also be factored into portfolio construction.

Finally, we have seen that credit spread exposure can be an important contributor to the equity beta of a portfolio, particularly in periods of stress, when the volatility of spreads increases dramatically. It is therefore crucial that investors realistically assess the likelihood of an economic contraction and not focus on too narrow a historical window when calibrating their outlook for the riskiness of credit spreads. Quiescent periods of persistent expansion can give way to financial disruption and recession over a relatively short period of time. It is often only in retrospect that the potential for contraction seems obvious. Since investors are most averse to losses in recessions, they should carefully consider whether they are being adequately compensated for the nonlinear equity beta embedded in their credit exposures.

Appendix A.3.

A.3.1. Measurement of Factors for Exhibits 3.1, 3.3, 3.10, 3.11, 3.12a, and 3.12b The volatility estimates reported in the exhibits under the heading "Return on a Broad Equity Index" are for the annualized standard deviation of monthly excess returns over short-term interest rates on a broad-based US equity market index (described in item A.3.2, below). The volatility estimates reported under the heading "Investment-Grade Credit Spread Return" are for the annualized standard deviation of the excess returns of a broad investment-grade credit index (over duration-matched Treasuries) *per year of duration* (described in item A.3.2, below).

The volatility estimates for US Treasury yield factors are computed as follows.

The volatilities reported under the headings "2-Year Treasury Return" and "10-Year Treasury Return" are the annualized standard deviations of monthly excess returns over the short-term riskless rate (*per unit of duration*) on (hypothetical) 2-year and 10-year par Treasury securities. Returns on hypothetical par Treasury securities of various maturities are estimated using data on constant-maturity Treasury yields provided by the Federal Reserve Board.

The volatility reported under the heading "5-Year × 5-Year Treasury Return" is the annualized standard deviation of monthly returns on a (hypothetical) 5-year forward contract on a 5-year par Treasury security (*per unit of duration of the forward contract*). These returns, in turn, are estimated as the difference between the excess return over the short rate on 10-year par Treasuries and the excess return over the short rate on 5-year Treasuries.

Returns on both legs are expressed *per unit of duration of the forward contract.* Both legs represent self-financed positions.

The volatility reported under the heading "10- to 20-Year Steepener Return" is the annualized standard deviation of monthly returns on a duration-neutral 10- to 20-year steepener position. This steepener position is constructed as a portfolio of a 1-year long duration position in a (hypothetical) 10-year par Treasury security, matched by a 1-year short duration position in a 20-year par Treasury security. Each leg of this trade is constructed to be self-financed (i.e., returns of each leg are measured over the short-term riskless rate). As a result, the steepener position is insulated against parallel movements in the curve—but is exposed to changes in its slope. It is a position designed to profit when the yield curve steepens.

Volatility estimates reported for currencies (yen and euro) are annualized standard deviations of estimated excess returns (over the US dollar short rate) on short-term yen and euro deposits. Before the advent of the euro, returns on the German mark are used.

The correlation estimates reported in Exhibits 3.10–3.13b are pairwise correlations of the time series described above.

Over short horizons, the excess returns (per unit of duration) that we have used are approximately equal to the *negative* of changes in the respective yields, credit spreads, and slope. It is, however, more accurate to use data on returns to estimate risk parameters—which is why we work with time series based on total and excess returns, rather than using time series of yield changes, spread changes, or slope changes.

A.3.2. Data Sources for Exhibits 3.1, 3.3, 3.10, 3.11, 3.12a, 3.12b, 3.13a, and 3.13b
For the period 1955–1969, the return on a broad US equity index is taken to be that of the market factor from the data library of Kenneth French. For the period 1970–1987, returns on US equities correspond to those of the MSCI USA Index. After 1988, returns on US equities are the returns to the S&P 500.

Historical returns to hypothetical par Treasury securities for various maturities are estimated from constant-maturity yields provided by the Federal Reserve Board. The H.15 series of constant-maturity Treasury yields is used for the period 1955–1961 for Treasuries 2 years and 5 years to maturity and for the period 1955–1971 for Treasuries 10 years to maturity. The long-bond yield from Ibbotson Associates is used for Treasury yields for securities 20 years to maturity until 1981. Thereafter, par rates provided by Gurkaynak, Sack, and Wright (2006) are used until 1996. After 1996, the 2-year, 5-year,

10-year, and 20-year Treasury return series are spliced with returns to the Barclays US Treasury 1–3 Years Index, the Barclays US Treasury 3–5 Years Index, the Barclays US Treasury 7–10 Years Index, and the Barclays US Long Treasury Index, respectively.

Excess returns to Treasuries and equities prior to 1988 are computed using the effective federal funds rate. For the period 1988–2001, excess returns are computed relative to 1-month LIBOR less 5 bps, to adjust for the average credit spread embedded in LIBOR. From 2002 on, excess returns are computed versus the 1-month overnight index swap (OIS) rate.

Credit returns start in 1973 and are based on the Barclays US Credit Index. This is a broad index of US investment-grade credit bonds. Excess returns of the index are over a portfolio of duration-matched Treasuries. After January 1988, these excess returns are as reported by Barclays. Prior to January 1988, we estimate these excess returns by subtracting from the total return on the US (investment-grade) Credit Index (as reported by Barclays) the total return on a portfolio of US Treasuries that is duration and value matched with the credit index.

Excess returns to the yen and the euro are versus the US dollar and start in February 1975. From 2005 on, excess returns to the yen and the euro are computed using 1-month forwards. Before 2005, returns to JPY/USD and EUR/USD are computed using percentage changes in the spot exchange rate plus the carry from short-term interest rate differentials. Prior to the introduction of the euro in 1999, we use returns on the German mark. For the euro, the short-term interest rate is the overnight money market rate (from Haver Analytics) until May 1979, the German repo rate (14-day) from June 1979 to October 1989, the 1-month German mark LIBOR from November 1989 to November 1998, and the 3-month euro deposit rate from December 1998 to December 2004. For the Japanese yen, the short-term interest rate is the central bank discount rate (from Haver Analytics) until November 1985 and the 3-month yen LIBOR from December 1985 to December 2004.

A.3.3. Estimating the Level Dependence of the Volatility of Treasury Yield Changes (Results in Exhibit 3.6) We use the following equation for results reported in Exhibit 3.6:

$$R_{t,t+\Delta t}^i = \alpha_i + \sigma_t^i \cdot \left(y_t^i\right)^\gamma \cdot z_{t,t+\Delta t}^i,$$

where $R_{t,t+\Delta t}^i$ is the excess return of a US Treasury bond of maturity i between times t and $t + \Delta t$ per unit of duration at time t, y_t^i is the yield of a US

Treasury bond of maturity i at time t, σ_t^i is the volatility of a function of rates, and $z_{t,t+\Delta t}^i$ is a random variable with unit variance. The constant γ controls the degree of level dependence of volatility: When $\gamma = 0$, there is no level dependence, and volatility scales linearly with the level of rates when $\gamma = 1$.

The metric of the effectiveness of different values of γ is computed as follows. First, define "normalized yield changes" by

$$N_{t+\Delta t}^i \equiv \frac{R_{t,t+\Delta t}^i}{\hat{\sigma}_t^i \cdot \left(y_t^i\right)^\gamma},$$

where $\hat{\sigma}_t^i$ is the estimate of the volatility of the rates factor in the historical sample ending at time t. Then, the goodness of the model is judged by the proximity of the standard deviation of N_t^i to 1 across the range of various relevant maturities.

A.3.4. Estimating the Mean Reversion in Volatility (Results in Exhibits 3.8 and 3.9) To estimate the mean reversion in the volatility of equity returns and 10-year Treasury yield changes, we assume that

$$\sigma_t^i - \bar{\sigma}_t^i = \alpha_i + \beta_i\left(\sigma_{t-k}^i - \bar{\sigma}_{t-k}^i\right) + \varepsilon_t^i,$$

where σ_t^i is the realized volatility of the returns of asset $i\left[i \in (UST\ 10y,\ S\&P\ 500)\right]$ over the 1-month period ending at date t, $\bar{\sigma}_t^i$ is the realized volatility of asset i over the 5-year period ending at date t, and k denotes the lag length. We consider lag lengths of 1, 3, 6, and 12 months.

A.3.5. Estimating the Equity Beta of Credit Excess Returns (Results in Exhibit 3.17) The equity betas of credit excess returns reported in the second panel of Exhibit 3.17 use credit excess returns per unit of duration times the trailing 12-month average spread. Our specification is as follows:

$$\frac{R_{t+1}^i}{D_t^i.\bar{S}_t^i} = \alpha_i + \beta_i.R_{t+1}^{eq} + \varepsilon_{t+1}^i,$$

where R_{t+1}^i is the excess return of credit bucket $i\left[i \in (Aa,A,...)\right]$ between times t and $t + 1$, D_t^i is the spread duration of the bucket at time t, $\bar{S}_t^i$ is the trailing

12-month average option-adjusted spread (OAS) of the bucket ending at time t, and R_{t+1}^{eq} is the excess return of the S&P 500 Index over cash between times t and $t + 1$.

A.3.6. Estimating the Equity Beta of Credit Excess Returns in Up Markets and Down Markets (Results in Exhibit 3.18)
To estimate the up-market and down-market betas of credit excess returns, we use the following equation:

$$\frac{R_{t+1}^i}{D_t^i.S_t^i} = \alpha_i + \alpha_{down}^i.1_{R_{t+1}^{eq}<0} + \beta_{up}^i.R_{t+1}^{eq}.1_{R_{t+1}^{eq}>0} + \beta_{down}^i.R_{t+1}^{eq}.1_{R_{t+1}^{eq}<0} + \varepsilon_{t+1}^i,$$

where $i \in (Rating\ buckets\ Aa, A,..., Maturity\ buckets\ 1-3yr, 3-5yr)$, and $1_{R_{t+1}^{eq}>0}$ is the indicator variable that takes the value of 1 when S&P 500 excess returns are positive and zero otherwise. Similarly, $1_{R_{t+1}^{eq}<0}$ is the indicator variable that takes the value of 1 when S&P 500 excess returns are negative and zero otherwise. Other quantities are as defined previously.

Appendix B.3.

B.3.1. A Macro Factor Model for the Stock–Bond Correlation
We focus on modeling yields (bond yields and equity earnings yields), as opposed to returns, for econometric convenience.[11] Equations 3.1 and 3.2 show the model dynamics we assume for the 10-year US Treasury yield, y_b:

$$y_b(t) = \alpha_b + \beta_1 g(t) + \beta_2 u(t) + \beta_3 \pi(t) + \delta_b(t), \tag{3.1}$$

$$\Delta y_b(t) = \rho_b \delta_b(t-1) + \gamma_1 \Delta g(t) + \gamma_2 \Delta u(t) + \gamma_3 \Delta \pi(t) + \varepsilon_b(t), \tag{3.2}$$

where g is expected 1-year US GDP growth from the Survey of Professional Forecasters (SPF) of the Federal Reserve Bank of Philadelphia, u is the US unemployment rate, and π is expected 1-year inflation in the United States (from SPF). All variables in our model are expressed as deviations from their full sample averages; hence, we refer to them as unemployment gap, growth

---

[11]We note that the correlation of returns is very close to the correlation of changes in valuations and yields, since valuation changes dominate returns. For instance, even at the 2-year horizon, stock returns have a correlation greater than 95% with changes in cyclically adjusted earnings yields. And for Treasuries, the correlation between realized returns and changes in yields is even tighter. Hence, for the purposes of estimating the stock–bond correlation, using changes in valuations is roughly equivalent to using returns.

gap, and inflation gap. A positive gap means that the variable is higher than its average over the full sample. The long-run relationships between bond yields and the macro variables are determined by Equation 3.1. The short-run dynamics are governed by Equation 3.2, which includes an "error correction" component that drives the variables towards long-term equilibrium (Equation 3.1).

Similarly, the dynamics for equity yields, $y_e(t)$, are given by Equations 3.3 and 3.4:

$$y_e(t) = \alpha_e + \theta_1 g(t) + \theta_2 u(t) + \theta_3 \pi(t) + \delta_e(t), \tag{3.3}$$

$$\Delta y_e(t) = \rho_e \delta_e(t-1) + \varphi_1 \Delta g(t) + \varphi_2 \Delta u(t) + \varphi_3 \Delta \pi(t) + \varepsilon_e(t). \tag{3.4}$$

For earnings yield, we use the cyclically adjusted earnings yield (CAEY) from Robert Shiller's website. We calibrate our model on quarterly data starting in Q1 1988 and ending in Q2 2013.

Exhibit 3.20a and **3.20b** report our parameter estimates alongside *t*-statistics in both the level regression and the error correction models. As expected, the coefficients on the business cycle variables (real GDP growth and unemployment) have opposite signs for bond and equity earnings yields, in terms of both levels and changes. For example, in the regression based on changes, a 1% increase in real GDP growth would increase the yield on the 10-year Treasury bond by 51 bps and decrease earnings yields by 51 bps (stock prices would increase). Hence, when real growth or real business cycle shocks dominate the macroeconomic environment, as has been the case recently, we can expect a negative stock–bond correlation. By contrast, the coefficients on inflation in the levels equations have the same sign for

Exhibit 3.20a. Error Correction Model (ECM) Results

Level Regression	Nominal 10-Year Yield			Earnings Yield		
Variable	Coefficient	Value	*t*-Stat	Coefficient	Value	*t*-Stat
Constant	α_b	0.054	60.45	α_e	0.04	86.67
GDP growth	β_1	0.15	0.99	θ_1	−0.34	−3.40
Unemployment	β_2	−0.27	−4.38	θ_2	0.50	13.10
Inflation	β_3	1.99	16.85	θ_3	0.98	13.46
R^2		80%			79%	

Notes: As of 31 December 2015. [Historical data from Q1 1988 to Q2 2013.]
Source: PIMCO.

Exhibit 3.20b.   Error Correction Model (ECM) Results

Changes Regression		Nominal 10-Year Yield			Earnings Yield		
Variable		Coefficient	Value	*t*-Stat	Coefficient	Value	*t*-Stat
Δ GDP growth	γ_1		0.51	3.43	ϕ_1	−0.51	−4.93
Δ Unemployment	γ_2		−0.18	−1.09	ϕ_2	0.27	2.18
Δ Inflation	γ_3		0.70	2.50	ϕ_3	−0.20	−0.93
ECM	ρ_b		−0.17	−3.06	ρ_e	−0.17	−2.37
R^2			20%			29%	

Notes: As of 31 December 2015. [Historical data from Q1 1988 to Q2 2013.]
Source: PIMCO.

stocks and bonds, based on the long-run level dynamics. Thus, when inflation shocks become a relatively larger driver of risk, we would expect a more positive stock–bond correlation. Next, we use this model to derive correlations between bonds and equities.

  ▨ *Forward-looking correlations.* **Exhibit 3.21** illustrates the multistep process we use to generate model-implied bond–equity correlations. We follow three broad steps. First, we simulate a thousand paths for growth, unemployment, and inflation. Second, we derive a thousand simulated paths in stock and bond yields, based on our econometric model (using the coefficients on levels and changes from Exhibit 3.20). Finally, from these simulated changes, we calculate the stock–bond correlation at various time horizons.

  To simulate the behavior of key macroeconomic variables, we use projected Federal Open Market Committee (FOMC) data as mean outcomes for each variable.[12] The annual projections as of June 2013 are shown in **Exhibit 3.22**, alongside summary sample statistics for the macroeconomic variables.

Exhibit 3.21.   Process to Derive Forward-Looking Correlations

Simulate paths for macro variables	→	For each path, calculate implied stocks and bond yield changes	→	Derive implied stock–bond correlation

[12]Annual forecasts are interpolated linearly to obtain quarterly values. The gaps are estimated as differences from the sample average (Q1 1988–Q2 2013).

Exhibit 3.22. FOMC Projections and Historical Data for Macroeconomic Variables

	Real GDP growth	Unemployment	Inflation rate
FOMC Projections			
2013	2.45%	7.25%	1.00%
2014	3.25%	6.65%	1.70%
2015	3.35%	6.00%	1.80°%
Gaps			
2013	-0.22%	1.20%	-1.46%
2014	0.58%	0.60%	-0.76%
2015	0.68%	-0.05%	-0.66%
Historical Data (Q1 1988 to Q2 2013)			
Mean Levels	2.67%	6.05%	2.46%
Min	0.79%	3.90%	1.30%
Max	4.01%	9.90%	4.66%
Std. deviation	0.61%	1.58%	0.81%
Mean Changes	0.01%	-0.06%	-0.02%
Min	-0.93%	-2.00%	-0.66%
Max	1.10%	1.00%	0.37%
Std. deviation	0.33%	0.52%	0.18%

Notes: As of 31 December 2015. Historical data from Q1 1988 to Q2 2013.
Sources: FOMC (data as of June 2013); Haver Analytics; Bloomberg; PIMCO.

We estimate the autocorrelation dynamics, the volatilities, and the correlations of these variables based on historical data from Q1 1988 to Q2 2013. To do so, we estimate a simple model for the changes in the macro variables (Δy_j), as shown below.

$$\Delta y_j(t) = \alpha \Delta y_j(t-1) + \beta y_j(t) + \varepsilon_j(t),$$

where j indexes the macro variable considered, α captures autocorrelation in changes and β captures mean reversion in levels. **Exhibit 3.23** shows our estimated parameters alongside the correlations and volatilities of the error terms (ε_j).

Exhibit 3.23. Parameter of Stochastic Processes for Macroeconomic Variables

	Correlations and Volatilities of ε's				Parameters	
	GDP	Unemp.	Infl.	Volatility	α	β
GDP	100%			0.6%	25%	−18%
Unemp.	−25%	100%		0.4%	71%	−3%
Infl.	−1%	−22%	100%	0.4%	6%	−4%

Notes: As of 31 December 2015. Data from Q1 1988 to Q2 2013.
Source: PIMCO.

The realizations of the driving macroeconomic variables are jointly simulated a thousand times for nine quarters, with the correlation and volatility structure dictated by the parameters in Exhibit 3.23 and average realizations along the path given by the FOMC projections in Exhibit 3.22.

4. Risk Premia in Financial Markets

From the risk dimension, we now move to an analysis of the reward dimension of the optimal risk–reward trade-off. The willingness to take systematic risk should earn a risk premium in competitive financial markets with risk-averse investors. In this chapter, we begin with the economic justification for the existence of factor risk premia and examine the behavior of realized risk premia of systematic risk factors over a long history. These risk factors include not just the market factor but a number of other "priced" systematic factors. A top-down asset allocation exercise aims to capture these risk premia while keeping the overall risk taken within an acceptable range. We also show that factor risk premia are not constant over time but vary over the business cycle. We argue that portfolio formation should attempt to take advantage of this cyclical variation by orienting the portfolio mix towards risky assets in the late stages of a recession and the early stages of an expansion and by reducing risk as expansions begin to mature. This, however, is easier said than done. Only a minority of asset managers are likely to be able to consistently profit from timing the business cycle.

4.1. Factor Risk Premia: Theoretical Underpinnings vs. Historical Experience

One of the fundamental principles of asset pricing is that risk-averse investors demand a risk premium for bearing economy-wide risk that cannot be diversified away. Procyclical risk factors, such as the broad equity market factor, which do badly in bad times, should earn a positive risk premium. Factors that do well in bad times should have *lower*—possibly even negative—expected returns (over the riskless rate), since investors ought to be willing to pay to get exposure to them. The magnitude of these excess returns should also be related to the degree of risk aversion among investors (i.e., their aversion to losses in bad economic conditions) and the degree of covariation of returns with aggregate wealth.

In **Exhibit 4.1**, we present empirical estimates of risk premia on key risk factors. These are computed as long-sample averages of realized returns (in excess of the short-term riskless rate in the case of equities and 20-year US Treasuries, and in excess of the returns on a duration-matched portfolio of US Treasuries in the case of investment-grade corporate bonds). We focus on US Treasuries, equities, and investment-grade corporate credit spreads because

Exhibit 4.1. Average Excess Returns and Sharpe Ratios of Key Risk Factors in the Long Sample

	US Treasuries (20- Year) (vs. cash)	US Equities (vs. cash)	US Investment-Grade Credit (vs. duration-matched Treasuries)
	1900–2015		
Average excess returns (% per year)	1.5	7.5	—
Volatility (% per year)	8.8	19.5	—
Sharpe ratio	0.17	0.38	—
	1955–2015		*1973–2015*
Average excess returns (% per year)	1.7	5.5	0.5
Volatility (% per year)	9.8	14.6	3.5
Sharpe ratio	0.18	0.38	0.13

Notes: As of 31 December 2015. For the first panel (1900–2015), US equity and Treasury excess returns use *annual* data from the Dimson–Marsh–Staunton (DMS) global database (1900–2013). This database contains annual returns on stocks, bonds, bills, inflation, and currencies for 21 countries and three regions from 1900 to 2013. See Dimson, Marsh, and Staunton (2013a, 2013b) for a detailed description of the methodology. Since 2014, equity returns are based on the MSCI USA Index and Treasury returns are based on returns to Barclays US Long Treasury Index. Excess returns are calculated over US Treasury bills. For factor definitions and data sources for the second panel, see notes to Exhibit 3.1a and the Appendix to Chapter 3 (items A.3.1 and A.3.2). These data are at monthly frequency.

Sources: Barclays; Bloomberg; data library of Kenneth French; Dimson–Marsh–Staunton (DMS) global database; Federal Reserve; Gurkaynak, Sack, and Wright (2006); Ibbotson Associates; MSCI; PIMCO.

they represent the bulk of the market portfolio and are the fundamental drivers of risk and returns for global portfolios.

Over the past 110 years, the average returns of US Treasuries and equities over cash have been positive—as have the average returns of the US investment-grade credit index over duration-matched Treasuries[13] over the past 40 years for which we have data. On a volatility-adjusted basis, US equities have outperformed both Treasuries and investment-grade credit. While the Sharpe ratio of US equities is close to 0.4 in the long sample, the Sharpe ratios of US Treasuries (over cash) and US investment-grade credit (over Treasuries) are close to 0.2 and 0.1, respectively.[14]

[13]As noted in Chapter 2, by using excess returns over duration-matched Treasuries, we are focusing on the return attributable to credit *spreads*. Accordingly, we use the terms "excess returns to IG credit over Treasuries" and "returns of credit spreads" interchangeably.

[14]See also Surz (2016), who reports an estimate of the Sharpe ratio of the S&P 500, linked with predecessor indices, of 0.34 over the 90-year period 1926–2015.

To examine whether this long-sample historical experience is consistent with economic theory, in **Exhibit 4.2**, we present the performance of US Treasuries, equities, and investment-grade credit in economic expansions and recessions. We use business cycle peaks and troughs as defined by the National Bureau of Economic Research (NBER). NBER dates are based on a broad set of indicators and are widely accepted as business cycle dates in the United States.

The returns to US equities and investment-grade credit spreads are procyclical: Historical average excess returns and Sharpe ratios are positive in expansions and negative in recessions. This behavior is consistent with the scenario in which financial markets price in impairments to dividends and increased corporate defaults at the onset of recessions and then reverse when the economy emerges from the depth of a recession. This procyclical behavior of returns on equities and investment-grade credit spreads is broadly consistent with the positive realized risk premium on these risk factors.

Exhibit 4.2. Average Excess Returns and Sharpe Ratios of Key Risk Factors in Recessions and Expansions

	US 10-Year Treasuries (vs. cash)	US Equities (vs. cash)	US Investment-Grade Credit (vs. duration-matched Treasuries)
	1955–2015		*1973–2015*
Expansions			
Average excess returns (% per year)	0.5	7.3	0.7
Sharpe ratio	0.08	0.55	0.28
Recessions			
Average excess returns (% per year)	6.2	−5.7	−1.2
Sharpe ratio	0.59	−0.28	−0.17

Notes: As of 31 December 2015. Recession dates are from NBER. For factor definitions and a full list of data sources, see notes to Exhibit 3.1a and the Appendix to Chapter 3 (items A.3.1 and A.3.2). Returns data are at monthly frequency.

Sources: Barclays; Bloomberg; data library of Kenneth French; Dimson–Marsh–Staunton (DMS) global database; Federal Reserve; Gurkaynak, Sack, and Wright (2006); Ibbotson Associates; MSCI; PIMCO.

Reconciling the Countercyclicality of Treasury Returns with Positive Risk Premia on Bonds The countercyclical properties of returns on US Treasuries are somewhat harder to reconcile with their outperformance in the long sample. US Treasuries outperform in recessions, with a Sharpe ratio of 0.6, and exhibit relative underperformance in expansions, with a Sharpe ratio close to zero. Such countercyclicality in returns would warrant a negative risk premium on Treasuries—because, as standard economic theory suggests, investors ought to pay, on average, for risk factors that outperform in periods of economic weakness.

Several partial explanations have been forwarded to explain this "anomaly." First, short-horizon returns to Treasuries and equities were positively correlated for much of this historical sample. The fact that US Treasuries had a small positive equity beta in this sample can potentially explain their outperformance. Second, inflation uncertainty exhibits a fairly strong level of dependency. The fact that inflation covaries predictably with real activity can lead to a positive risk premium on nominal government bonds under some restrictive assumptions (see Campbell, Sunderam, and Viceira 2013).

It can also be argued that an inflation risk premium was built into government bond yields for a considerable period of time after the experience of the Great Inflation of 1965–1985. The success of monetary policy in taming inflation was a surprise to the bond markets, and bonds continued to deliver positive excess returns. The hedging value of risk-free bonds was priced into the yield curve only after inflationary fears were definitively laid to rest in the late 1990s. This trend was reinforced by the entry of large emerging economies, such as China, into the global economic system and the resulting deflationary pressures. In light of these arguments, and as we have observed before, this extraordinary outperformance of government bonds may be unlikely to repeat.

The Equity Risk Premium "Puzzle" While the sign of the realized risk premium on equities is consistent with these assets' procyclical behavior, its magnitude has been the subject of debate. Mehra and Prescott (1985) observed that the 6%–8% equity risk premium observed on average historically in the United States is not compatible with standard macroeconomic models. They observed that the degree of investor risk aversion required to justify equity risk premia in the 6%–8% range would be extreme and inconsistent with the estimates of risk aversion obtained in other contexts.

A range of explanations has been offered for this inconsistency. As illustrated in **Exhibit 4.3**, the average excess return on global equities is somewhat lower than that on US equities—particularly if we include countries

87

Exhibit 4.3. Long-Sample Performance of Global Equity Markets: 1900–2015

	US	World ex US	Europe	Japan
Average excess return (% per year)	7.5	5.1	5.1	9.3
Volatility (% per year)	19.5	18.6	19.2	27.5
Sharpe ratio	0.38	0.27	0.26	0.34

Notes: As of 31 December 2015. These computations use annual data. See notes to Exhibit 4.1 (first panel) for details of the underlying data source. Returns data are at monthly frequency.
Sources: Bloomberg; DMS global database; PIMCO.

that have experienced significant negative economic shocks, such as Russia and Argentina. So a fraction of the "unduly high" equity risk premium has been attributed to the fact that the United States is a survivor economy.

Other risk-based explanations of the high equity risk premium involve modifying the structure of investors' preferences. (For example, investors become habituated to particular levels of consumption, which can lead to a highly nonlinear time variation in investor risk aversion; risk aversion can rise dramatically with the probability of recession.) As noted by Mehra (2008), while this puzzle is not fully resolved, research efforts in the direction of solving it have led to a vastly greater understanding of investors' preferences and the behavior of risk premia themselves. See also Mehra (2011).

Lower Sharpe Ratio of Investment-Grade Credit vs. Equities As seen in Exhibit 4.1, the Sharpe ratio of US equities far exceeds that of investment-grade credit index spreads. Considering that returns to credit spreads are markedly procyclical and have a pronounced negative skew, we might have expected a higher Sharpe ratio for credit, closer to that of equities. Another measure of this "underperformance" of investment-grade credit indices is the fact that the average excess return of such indices has consistently been lower than their average initial spreads, adjusted for default losses.

Ng and Phelps (2011) explain that a part of this slippage in performance is attributable to the definition of credit indices, which implicitly sell bonds when they are downgraded below investment grade or when they fall below one year of residual maturity. In addition, these indices also exclude bonds that do not satisfy certain liquidity criteria (mainly based on the size of issue). Ng and Phelps show that adjusting for these features would significantly enhance the estimate of average excess returns on investment-grade credit spreads.

4.2. Risk Premia in Interest Rates, Equities, and Credit Spreads: Beyond the Market Factor

In Chapter 2, we showed that factors in addition to the market significantly help explain the variance in returns on interest rates, equities, and credit markets. We now examine the performance properties of these factors and discuss possible economic reasons for these factors to be "priced"—that is, to command a positive (or negative) risk premium.

Interest Rate Risk Factors: Duration and Curve In **Exhibit 4.4**, we present the performance of US Treasuries by maturity. Here, excess returns are stated as returns *per year of duration*. As discussed above, over the past 60 years, bearing interest rate risk has earned a positive premium. Full sample estimates are, however, combinations of averages over two radically different interest rate regimes. Starting from a low of 2.61% per year at the beginning of 1955, the 10-year US Treasury yield peaked at above 15% per year in 1981, during the Volcker period of monetary policy tightening. In December 2015, this yield was back at 2.24% per year. Reflecting this experience, the Sharpe ratios of US Treasuries were in the range of 0.6–0.7 over the period since 1985 and were negative in the 30 years prior. A Sharpe ratio of 0.6 to 0.7 is a remarkably good performance—higher than that of equities over the long

Exhibit 4.4.   Performance of US Treasuries across the Curve, per Year of Duration, January 1955–December 2015

	US 2-Year Treasury	US 5-Year Treasury	US 10-Year Treasury	US 20-Year Treasury
1955–2015				
Average excess returns (% per year)	0.3	0.3	0.2	0.2
Volatility (% per year)	1.5	1.2	1.1	1.0
Sharpe ratio	0.22	0.23	0.19	0.18
Beta to US 10-year Treasury returns	1.14	1.07	1.00	0.87
Subsample Sharpe ratios				
1955–1984	−0.04	−0.12	−0.17	−0.16
1985–2015	0.71	0.67	0.60	0.57

Notes: As of 31 December 2015. For factor definitions and data sources, see notes to Exhibit 3.1a and the Appendix to Chapter 3 (items A.3.1 and A.3.2). Returns data are at monthly frequency.
Sources: Barclays; Bloomberg; Federal Reserve; Gurkaynak, Sack, and Wright (2006); Ibbotson Associates; PIMCO.

run. As shown in Exhibit 4.3, our estimate of the Sharpe ratio of US equities is 0.38 using data for the period 1900–2015.

Variations across maturities are also interesting. Sharpe ratios in the long sample are higher in short maturities, but they decline gently with maturity—2-year and 5-year Treasuries have a Sharpe ratio close to 0.22, while the Sharpe ratio of 20-year bonds was lower at 0.18. The differences in Sharpe ratios across maturities are more material in the post-1985 period, but the pattern of Sharpe ratios declining with maturity persists both in the rising-rate regime of 1955–1985 and in the falling-rate regime of 1985–2015.

As discussed in Chapter 2, we can characterize the dynamics of the yield curve as comprising three risk factors: a level, or duration, factor and two curve factors representing "steepener" positions in the front end and the long end of the curve. **Exhibit 4.5** presents the performance properties of the 5- to 10-year and 10- to 20-year steepeners, compared with 10-year US Treasury securities, over cash.[15] In effect, we restate the performance of bonds of various maturities shown in Exhibit 4.4 in terms of these steepener returns.

Both steepener positions exhibit positive average excess returns. This result is consistent with the pattern of Sharpe ratios declining with maturity, illustrated in Exhibit 4.4. Also, note that despite being duration neutral at inception, these returns have a positive beta (of roughly 0.1) to 10-year US Treasury returns.

The relative underperformance of the long end of the curve (20 years and above) has been attributed to "leverage aversion"—whereby leverage-constrained investors tend to bid up high-beta (i.e., long-duration) assets, making them structurally expensive (high prices, low yields) relative to shorter-duration assets. A preference for long-dated bonds among institutional investors with long-dated liabilities, such as defined benefit pension funds and life insurance companies, has also been suggested as a reason for the richness of long-maturity bonds. Considering that long-dated bonds have significantly higher convexity than short-dated ones, the average returns of the steepener trade can also be attributed to the volatility risk premium embedded in the pricing of the yield curve.

---

[15]Returns on 10-year Treasuries are expressed per year of duration in these calculations. As before, each steepener position is constructed as a portfolio of a 1-year long-duration position in a short-maturity bond, matched by a 1-year short-duration position in a long-maturity bond. Each leg of this trade is constructed to be self-financed (i.e., returns of each leg are measured over cash). Thus, the steepener position is insulated against parallel movements in the curve but is exposed to changes in its shape.

Exhibit 4.5. Performance of US Treasury Level and Curve Factors, January 1955–December 2015

	US 10-Year Treasuries	US 5-year to 10-Year Steepener	US 10-Year to 20-Year Steepener
1955–2015			
Average excess returns (% per year)	0.2	0.1	0.0
Volatility (% per year)	1.1	0.4	0.4
Sharpe ratio	0.19	0.20	0.07
Beta to US 10-year Treasuries	1.0	0.1	0.1
Subsample Sharpe ratios			
1955–1984	−0.17	0.10	−0.08
1985–2015	0.60	0.31	0.27

Notes: As of 31 December 2015. For factor definitions and data sources, see notes to Exhibit 3.1a and the Appendix to Chapter 3 (items A.3.1 and A.3.2). The 5- to 10-year steepener corresponds to a long position with 1-year of duration in 5-year Treasuries and a short position with 1-year of duration in 10-year Treasuries. Returns data are at monthly frequency.
Sources: Barclays; Bloomberg; Federal Reserve; Gurkaynak, Sack, and Wright (2006); Ibbotson Associates; PIMCO.

Equity Factors: Size, Value, and Momentum. A number of studies have presented evidence that there are priced risk factors (i.e., risk factors that carry a risk premium) in equity markets in addition to the broad market factor. The study of Fama and French (1992), which integrates earlier work by many researchers, is the most prominent one. These factors include a value factor (the so-called HML factor, defined as returns on a portfolio of stocks that is long high-book-to-market, or value, firms and short low-book-to-market firms) and a size factor (returns on a portfolio that is long small firms and short big firms, in market value terms, or SMB). Researchers have identified, in addition, that a momentum factor (returns on a portfolio that is long recent outperformers and short underperformers) also displays outperformance on average. The HML, SMB, and momentum factors all had positive average excess returns over the history shown in **Exhibit 4.6**. The outperformance of these factors has been the subject of intense debate—and has been attributed to features that can arise in models with rational forward-looking investors and also to those arising in the presence of investors who are subject to behavioral biases.

Exhibit 4.6. Historical Performance of Market, HML, SMB, and Momentum Factors, January 1955–December 2015

	Market	SMB	HML	Momentum
1955–2015				
Average excess returns (% per year)	5.5	2.3	3.9	8.8
Volatility (% per year)	14.6	10.2	9.5	14.0
Sharpe ratio	0.38	0.22	0.41	0.63
Beta to equity market	1.00	0.12	−0.16	−0.14
Subsample Sharpe ratios				
1955–1984	0.24	0.39	0.67	0.92
1985–2015	0.50	0.08	0.21	0.45

Notes: As of 31 December 2015. See notes to Exhibit 3.1a and the Appendix to Chapter 3 (items A.3.1 and A.3.2) for details of equity market returns. Returns of the SMB, HML, and momentum factors are from the data library of Kenneth French. The momentum factor is based on the prior 12 months of returns, excluding the most recent month (2–12). Returns data are at monthly frequency.
Sources: Data library of Kenneth French; PIMCO.

The HML factor overweights stocks with high book-to-market (B/M) ratios—that is, value stocks—which are thought by some to be riskier. Thus, the outperformance of the HML factor may simply represent compensation for bearing this risk. This explanation is supported only weakly by empirical evidence, considering that the beta of this factor to equity markets is negative (see Exhibit 4.6) and that this factor covaries weakly with the business cycle. Behavioral explanations, on the other hand, appeal to the possibility of the overreaction of stock prices to good or bad news—which can be exploited by a value-oriented strategy such as HML.

The performance of the SMB factor since 1955 has been a lot weaker than that of both the HML factor and the equity market factor (see Exhibit 4.6). Interestingly, the performance of the SMB factor in the first half of the sample far exceeds its performance in the past 30 years. This more recent weakness in performance has led to increased skepticism about SMB as a priced factor.

The returns to buying recent past winners and selling losers, introduced by Jegadeesh and Titman (1993) as the momentum factor, have been compelling. While this factor also shows a marked weakening in performance in the past 30 years (versus the first half of the sample since 1955), it has continued to offer positive returns on average. The outperformance of the momentum factor is difficult to explain in a framework with rational forward-looking investors, and many behavioral explanations of the phenomenon rely on barriers to quick information dissemination and underreaction by investors. Despite the lack of a satisfactory theoretical explanation, it is hard to ignore the momentum factor in portfolio construction, given its performance record (particularly in the early stages of recessions, as shown later).

Credit Spreads. In **Exhibit 4.7**, we present Sharpe ratios of credit (over duration-matched Treasuries) by rating and maturity buckets. Sharpe ratios of low-rated investment-grade and high-rated high-yield rating buckets are larger than those of the other buckets. More specifically, since 1988, Ba rated credit appears to be the sweet spot. As documented by Ben Dor and Xu (2011), the outperformance of this rating bucket versus others has been related to the "fallen angel" premium. Due to restrictions in investment mandates (effectively leading to investor segmentation), investors are often forced to sell credits when they are downgraded below investment grade—which leads to selling pressure on downgraded names. This exceptional spread widening often reverses, leading to a systematic outperformance of Ba rated bonds.

Sharpe ratios also monotonically decrease across maturity buckets. Strikingly, the Sharpe ratio of short-maturity credit (1–3 years) was close to 0.4 since 1973, while that of the 10+ years bucket was below 0.1. Several factors contribute to the outperformance of the front end of the credit curve. First, front-end credit buckets have a larger negative skew in their returns distribution than the long end—which is due to the front end's worse performance per unit of risk in periods of economic weakness. So the incremental performance can be thought of as compensation for bearing greater recession risk. Other explanations include the possibility of investor segmentation. For example, liability-driven investors tend to bid up—and perhaps overpay for—long corporate bonds in order to match their liabilities, which are discounted at corporate bond yields in many cases. (See, for example, Moore 2013.) Furthermore, the outperformance of short-maturity credit is not unlike the outperformance of short-maturity government bonds. This result can be related to the high versus low beta effect that comes from leverage-averse investors bidding up the prices of high-beta assets (Frazzini and Pedersen 2014).

We can also define two long–short risk factors, along the lines of the Fama–French equity factors, which are designed to capture the regularities observed across rating and maturity buckets. The *credit quality* factor is systematically long Baa rated credit and short Aa rated credit, and the *credit*

Exhibit 4.7. Sharpe Ratios of Credit (over Treasuries) by Rating and Maturity, January 1973–December 2015

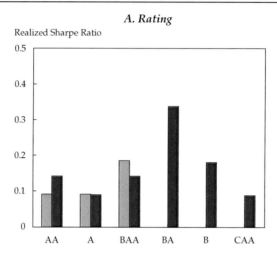

A. Rating

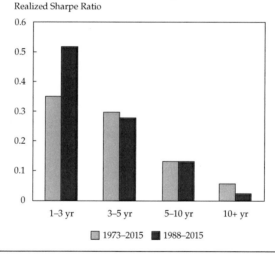

B. Maturity

Notes: As of 31 December 2015. Excess returns of various rating and maturity buckets of the credit market (over Treasuries) correspond to excess returns of various subindices of the Barclays US Credit Index and the Barclays Corporate High Yield Index. From 1988 on, excess returns over Treasuries correspond to published excess returns from Barclays. Prior to 1988, excess returns over Treasuries are estimated using the published total returns on these subindices and the total returns on a value- and duration-matched portfolio of Treasuries. The Treasury returns used prior to 1988 are described in the Appendix to Chapter 3 (items A.3.1 and A.3.2). Returns data are at monthly frequency.

Sources: Barclays POINT; Federal Reserve; PIMCO.

slope factor is long the 1–3 years bucket and short the 10+ years bucket. Both factors are defined to be spread duration neutral; they are therefore immune to parallel movements in the spread curve across quality and maturity buckets, respectively.

In **Exhibit 4.8**, we document the performance of these factors compared with constant exposure of *one year of spread duration* in the investment-grade credit index. As expected, all factors have positive average excess returns. Both the quality and slope factors retain a positive beta to the credit market and tend to have more negatively skewed returns distributions than the market. Both of these aspects can justify the average outperformance of these factors.

Exhibit 4.8. Historical Performance of Credit Market, Slope, and Quality Factors, January 1973–December 2015

	Credit Market	Credit Quality	Credit Slope
1973–1979/2015			
Average excess returns (% per year)	0.07	0.10	0.27
Volatility (% per year)	0.53	0.44	0.61
Sharpe ratio	0.13	0.23	0.44
Skew	−0.9	−1.8	−1.7
Beta to credit market	1	0.49	0.23
Subsample Sharpe ratios			
1973–1984	0.28	0.39	−0.12
1985–2012/2015	0.09	0.16	0.82

Notes: As of 31 December 2015. The credit market factor corresponds to the excess return on the Barclays US Credit Index per year of spread duration. The credit quality factor is long Baa rated credit versus Aa rated credit, and the credit slope factor is long the 1–3 years bucket versus the 10+ years bucket. Returns on each leg of these factors are excess returns on subindices of the Barclays US Credit Index per year of spread duration. From 1988 on, excess returns over Treasuries correspond to published excess returns from Barclays. Prior to 1988, excess returns over Treasuries are estimated using the published total returns on these subindices and the total returns on a value- and duration-matched portfolio of Treasuries. The Treasury returns used prior to 1988 are described in the Appendix to Chapter 3 (items A.3.1 and A.3.2). Returns data are at monthly frequency.

Sources: Barclays POINT; Federal Reserve; PIMCO.

4.3. Cyclical Variations in Risk Premia

We have so far focused on the unconditional properties of risk premia, and we have suggested their performance in recessions as a justification for these risk factors' long-term averages being positive. However, this is not to suggest that risk premia are constant over time. In **Exhibit 4.9**, we present the Sharpe ratios of US 10-year Treasuries, US equities, and US investment-grade credit (over Treasuries) estimated over various stages of the NBER definition of the US business cycle. As before, we estimate Sharpe ratios in recessions and expansions, as well as in calendar halves of expansions. Analyzing the performance of risk factors in early versus late stages (the first half versus the second half) of expansions is instructive, as it reveals the relative performance of these factors as expansions mature and eventually give way to economic downturns.

As discussed above, equities and credit spreads (over Treasuries) covary positively with the business cycle. US Treasuries have the reverse property. There are, however, some nuances relating to the performance of these risk factors in the first and second halves of expansions. US Treasuries have outperformed cash in the early stages of expansions—coincident with an easy monetary policy regime and slack in the economy. It is only when expansions mature, and arguably as monetary policy is tightened, that US Treasuries underperform.

Exhibit 4.9. Sharpe Ratios of Equities, Rates, and Credit over the Business Cycle

	US 10-Year Treasuries (over cash)	US Equities (over cash)	US Investment-Grade Credit (over Treasuries)
Period	1955–2015		1973–2015
Unconditional (full sample)	0.19	0.38	0.13
Recessions	0.59	−0.28	−0.17
Expansions	0.05	0.55	0.28
1st half expansions	0.45	0.86	0.47
2nd half expansions	−0.48	0.21	−0.08

Notes: As of 31 December 2015. Recession dates are from NBER. First and second halves of expansions correspond to calendar halves of NBER expansions. For factor definitions and data sources, see notes to Exhibit 3.1a and the Appendix to Chapter 3 (items A.3.1 and A.3.2). Returns data are at monthly frequency.
Sources: Barclays; Bloomberg; data library of Kenneth French; Federal Reserve; Gurkaynak, Sack, and Wright (2006); Ibbotson Associates; MSCI; PIMCO.

Performance of Equities and Credit in Expansions. Equities outperform throughout expansions, but they exhibit a substantial weakening in performance in the late stages of expansions. The outperformance of credit-risky bonds in expansions is almost entirely restricted to the expansion's early stages. This divergence can potentially be linked to the behavior of corporate management in this stage of the business cycle. In **Exhibit 4.10,** we present some evidence from the last 60 years of history relating to US nonfinancial corporations.

As expansions mature, corporate profit growth tends to slow significantly (in comparison to the early stages of expansions), posing the risk of a decline in equity prices. In anticipation of this effect, corporate management teams have incentives to take shareholder-friendly actions at the expense of bondholders. They begin to compensate shareholders by increasing cash yields, in the form of either increased dividends or share buybacks, hoping for an expansion in price/EBITDA multiples. The increase in cash yields to shareholders is often financed by depleting cash from the balance sheet or by raising additional debt, which leads to an expansion of net debt and leverage—and eventually to a deterioration in credit quality. This chain of events contributes to the underperformance of credit markets in mature expansions.

Exhibit 4.10. US Nonfinancial Corporate Fundamentals, March 1955–December 2015

1955–2015	EBITDA Growth (quarter over quarter, % per year)	Dividend Yield (% per year)	Equity Price/ EBITDA	Net Debt Growth (quarter over quarter, % per year)	Change in Leverage (quarter over quarter, % per year)
Recessions	−4.4	3.6	4.2	6.6	2.4
Expansions	8.4	3.1	4.9	7.9	0.6
Early expansions	10.2	3.1	4.8	6.3	−0.7
Late expansions	6.0	2.9	5.0	10.0	2.2

Notes: As of 31 December 2015. First and second halves of expansions correspond to calendar halves of NBER expansions.
Sources: Federal Reserve Statistical Release Z.1, Financial Accounts of the United States; NBER.

Cyclical Performance of Other Risk Factors in Rate, Equity, and Credit Markets. In **Exhibit 4.11**, we present the Sharpe ratios of duration-neutral 5- to 10-year and 10- to 20-year steepener positions in US Treasuries, conditional on the stage of the business cycle. Despite the fact that the beta of these factors to returns of US 10-year Treasuries was low—only about 0.1—their performance over the cycle is quite similar to that of 10-year Treasuries: Outperformance is largely restricted to recessions, and the positions underperform in late-stage expansions. This result is consistent with the observation that the yield curve stays steep through the early stages of expansions and flattens noticeably only as monetary policy tightening gets under way in late expansions.

Exhibit 4.11. Sharpe Ratios of Rate Factors over the Business Cycle, January 1955–December 2015

	US 10-Year Treasuries	US 5- to 10-Year Steepener	US 10- to 20-Year Steepener
Unconditional (full sample)	0.19	0.20	0.07
Recessions	0.59	0.67	0.41
Expansions	0.05	0.07	−0.02
1st half expansions	0.45	0.27	0.17
2nd half expansions	−0.48	−0.25	−0.22

Notes: As of 31 December 2015. For factor definitions and data sources, see notes to Exhibit 3.1a and the Appendix to Chapter 3 (items A.3.1 and A.3.2). The 5- to 10-year steepener corresponds to a (self-financed) long position with one year of duration in the 5-year Treasury and a (self-financed) short position with one year of duration in the 10-year Treasury. First and second halves of expansions correspond to calendar halves of NBER expansions. Returns data are at monthly frequency.

Sources: Barclays; Bloomberg; Federal Reserve; Gurkaynak, Sack, and Wright (2006); Ibbotson Associates; NBER; PIMCO.

Risk factors in equity markets also exhibit variations in performance over the business cycle, as illustrated in **Exhibit 4.12**. Both the SMB (small minus big) factor and the HML (high B/M minus low B/M) factor have similar Sharpe ratios in recessions and expansions; as previously mentioned, this apparent lack of cyclicality represents a challenge to efforts to theoretically justify the risk premia earned by these factors. The momentum factor, on the other hand, underperforms in recessions relative to expansions. However, its underperformance is concentrated in the late stages of recessions as stock valuations come past their trough. There is a break in

Exhibit 4.12. Sharpe Ratios of Equity Factors over the Business Cycle, January 1955–December 2015

	Market	SMB	HML	Momentum
Unconditional (full sample)	0.38	0.22	0.41	0.63
Recessions	−0.28	0.24	0.43	0.11
Expansions	0.55	0.22	0.41	0.80
1st half recessions	−1.80	−0.45	1.65	0.84
2nd half recessions	0.68	0.84	−0.47	−0.32
1st half expansions	0.86	0.34	0.62	0.70
2nd half expansions	0.21	0.13	0.21	0.91

Notes: As of 31 December 2015. See notes to Exhibit 3.1a and the Appendix to Chapter 3 (items A.3.1 and A.3.2) for details of equity market returns. Returns of the SMB, HML, and momentum factors are from the data library of Kenneth French. Recession dates are from NBER. First and second halves of recessions and expansions correspond to calendar halves of NBER recessions and expansions. Returns data are at monthly frequency.
Sources: Data library of Kenneth French; NBER; PIMCO.

the trend of stock prices in these periods, and momentum-based investing, which relies on trend continuation for its success, underperforms. In early recessions, the momentum factor retains its outperformance.

As we partition the historical record into calendar halves of business cycles, we find that the SMB and HML factors outperform more strongly in early-stage expansions than in late-stage expansions. The relative weakening of performance of the HML factor in late expansions is at least weakly consistent with the notion that its performance covaries positively with the economic cycle. One possible reason for this behavior is that firms with high book-to-market ratios tend to have significant amounts of assets in place, which reduces their flexibility in responding to economic downturns (Zhang 2005). The SMB and HML factors perform differently in early and late stages of recessions. The outperformance of HML in early-stage recessions and underperformance in late-stage recessions points to overshooting in the valuation of low-book-to-market stocks; by contrast, the SMB factor underperforms in early recessions, along with the overall market.

In **Exhibit 4.13**, we present the performance of the credit quality and slope factors. Strikingly, both factors perform similarly to the credit market factor over different stages of the business cycle. The quality and slope factors both underperform in recessions and in late expansions versus early

Exhibit 4.13. Sharpe Ratios of Credit Factors over the Business Cycle, January 1973–December 2015

	Credit Market (over Treasuries)	Credit Quality	Credit Slope
Unconditional (full sample)	0.13	0.23	0.44
Recessions	−0.17	−0.21	−0.13
Expansions	0.28	0.46	0.80
1st half expansions	0.47	0.74	0.94
2nd half expansions	−0.08	−0.12	0.59

Notes: As of 31 December 2015. See Exhibit 4.8 for methodology and sources. Recession dates are from NBER. First and second halves of expansions correspond to calendar halves of NBER expansions. Returns data are at monthly frequency.
Sources: Barclays; NBER; PIMCO.

expansions. The cyclicality of the slope factor is consistent with the notion that relative outperformance of the front end of the credit curve is in part attributable to higher jump-to-default risk, which is heightened in periods of economic weakness.

4.4. Lessons for Asset Allocation

There are reasonably well-identified systematic risk factors in financial markets that earn a risk premium, and these risk premia are time varying. We have argued that the stage of the business cycle matters for assessing risk premia. A top-down asset allocation exercise would benefit from an assessment of the current stage of the economic cycle and how it might change over the decision horizon. However, the exercise of predicting the business cycle is necessarily a hard one, and not all portfolio managers may be skilled at it. Just the fact that risk premia follow predictable patterns over the business cycle does not imply that all investors are able to exploit these predictable variations successfully.

The analysis of both unconditional and conditional risk premia presented above provides guidelines regarding the Sharpe ratio inputs investors can use for asset allocation. While one should take heed of the old adage that "past performance is no guarantee of future results," investors should also be cautious of accepting the argument that "this time is different." The evidence that there are a number of risk factors other than the market factor that earn a risk premium implies that the optimal portfolio should carefully balance exposures to all these risk factors. The task of constructing such an optimal portfolio involves careful judgment about whether a particular factor is a genuine systematic factor that will reliably earn a risk premium in the future or whether it is just a short-lived anomaly or, worse still, an artifact of data mining.

5. Valuations and Risk Premia

We have shown in the previous chapter that risk premia vary systematically with the business cycle. However, which stage of the cycle the economy is in is not known in real time with certainty. Asset prices continuously reflect changing assessments by investors about the current state of the economy and its future evolution. In this process, time-varying risk premia become embedded in asset prices. Prices themselves contain information about risk premia: Holding other things constant, prices should be lower if risk premia are high and vice versa. Asset allocators may infer some of this information about risk premia from prices and use it in allocation decisions. However, other things are hardly ever constant. Asset prices may be lower because expectations of cash flows have fallen and not because risk premia have increased. A portfolio rebalancing would be in order only if price declines are coming from an increase in the expected return premium per unit of risk.

The task of separating changes in cash flow expectations from changes in risk premia is, however, subject to substantial imprecision. Expectations of cash flows, risk aversion, risk, and the price of risk are all unobservable quantities that cannot be accurately inferred from market prices alone. Even so, an active investment style that does not consider valuations is hard to defend as reasonable. In this chapter, we discuss some standard *valuation metrics* that are used in equity and bond markets. We review the evidence that valuation metrics such as price-to-earnings ratios (P/Es) and bond yields have some predictive power in forecasting returns. We show that while simple valuation metrics are generally informative of risk premia (both in the cross section and over time), they must be employed with care. Measures such as the cyclically adjusted P/E (CAPE) ratio can drift for long periods of time away from their long-run averages, posing significant challenges to their use in value-driven investment strategies.

5.1. Excess Volatility and the Promise of Value

Fundamental asset-pricing equations link valuation metrics to expected returns. For example, a higher dividend yield in equities must correspond to either higher expected returns or lower expected dividend growth. In a simplified setting, consider first the Gordon and Shapiro (1956) growth model, as shown below:

$$\frac{D}{P} = (r + \lambda) - g,$$

where D is the current dividend, r is the long risk-free real rate, λ is the equity risk premium, and g is the real long-term expected dividend growth rate.

The dividend yield is higher when expected returns are higher and when expected growth is lower. As shown in Campbell and Shiller (1988) and as we demonstrated in Chapter 3, the observed variation in the dividend yield is too large to be accounted for by volatility in dividend growth alone. Thus, a large part of the variation in valuation indicators such as the dividend yield ought to come from variations in the equity risk premium.

There are many possible explanations for the excessive volatility of asset prices. One hypothesis is that households' demand for liquidity accentuates fundamental risks, especially during recessions. In **Exhibit 5.1**, we present historical average flows of equities during NBER recessions over the period 1952–2015 by investor type (as a percentage of the beginning-of-period market value).

During recessions, households have sold 2.8% of their initial holdings, composing 1.9% of the total value of equities. Historically in the United States, defined-benefit pension funds have accommodated a large part of this flow (roughly 1% of the total value of equities). However, considering that the size of these pension funds' asset portfolio is a lot smaller than that of households, this purchase of equities represents a large portfolio shift (a roughly 11.8% increase in their equity allocation). In order to provide an incentive for such large portfolio adjustments, institutional investors demand a concession in the form of sharply higher risk premia in periods of economic weakness. In our view, these flows play an important role in generating higher volatility in asset prices than is justified by economic fluctuations.

Excess volatility in asset prices can present opportunities for active, value-driven investors if that volatility is accompanied by evidence of mean reversion in valuations. Indeed, implicit in the hypothesis that institutional investors demand a concession for providing liquidity to households in recessions is the view that institutional investors are value oriented—that is, that

103

Exhibit 5.1.   Equity Flows in Recessions, 1952–2015

A. Average Annualized Sector Equity Flows (1952–2015)

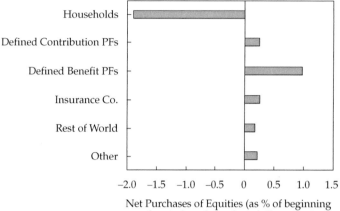

Net Purchases of Equities (as % of beginning
of period market value of all equities)

B. Net Purchases of Equities as % of Beginning of Period Market Value of Equities Held by Households and Defined Benefit Pension Plans

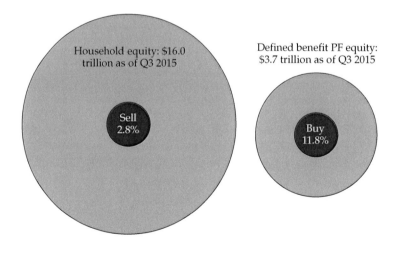

Notes: As of 31 December 2015. Figures in Panel B are not drawn to scale.
Sources: Federal Reserve Statistical Release Z.1, Financial Accounts of the United States; NBER.

they purchase equities in recessions with the expectation that valuations will revert to more normal levels.

To see whether there is empirical support for this interpretation of the data, consider a regression of equity returns on contemporaneous and lagged flows, as follows:

$$\text{Return}(t) = \alpha + \beta_1.flow(t) + \beta_2.avgflow(t-1) + \beta_3.RecessionDummy(t) + \varepsilon(t).$$

For robustness, we perform the analysis on two different sets of data: quarterly data on household sector asset flows from the Federal Reserve's Financial Accounts of the United States (Statistical Release Z.1) and monthly data from EPFR Global[16] on fund flows for US equity mutual funds marketed to retail investors. The results of this regression, presented in **Exhibit 5.2**, are consistent with risk premia increasing in order to motivate other investors to absorb households' asset sales in a downturn.

In particular, we find that estimates of β_1 are positive while estimates of β_3 are negative, indicating that household selling and outflows from retail equity mutual funds are associated with more negative returns, beyond those associated with a typical recession. Interestingly, there is some evidence of reversals, as seen in the negative estimate of β_2 in the higher-frequency regression using mutual fund data. Here, equities are expected to rebound after a month in which retail funds experience net outflows.

Although the results generally support the idea that risk premia adjust to accommodate household demand for liquidity, it must be cautioned that causality can run the other way. This is particularly true of the contemporaneous relationship between returns and flows, as exceptionally negative asset class performance may drive outflows.

Part of the reason the evidence of reversion in Exhibit 5.2 is weak is that asset prices tend to mean-revert somewhat slowly over periods longer than a year. In **Exhibit 5.3**, we present estimates of volatility of US equities, Treasury yields, and credit spreads, along with the ratio of variances estimated over long horizons to those over a 1-month horizon. In most cases, variance estimates decline sharply over 3- to 5-year horizons, which is indicative of mean reversion in asset prices over these horizons. Interestingly, the variance estimates decline little for the S&P 500 in the full sample, but they decrease markedly if we exclude the last 20 years. This result is due to a sustained decline in equity earnings yields in recent history, an important development that we revisit below.

---

[16]EPFR Global is a provider of data on global mutual fund flows. It is a part of the Financial Intelligence Division of Informa Business Intelligence, Inc.

Exhibit 5.2. Regression of Equity Returns on Contemporaneous and Lagged Flows, 1953–2015

	Long-Sample Evidence US Financial Accounts data 1953–December 2015	Higher-Frequency Evidence EPFR retail flows data 2003–December 2015
Same-period household flows into equities (β_1)	3.4**	2.4**
Trailing 1-year average of lagged household flows into equities (β_2)	−1.5	−2.5*
Recession indicator (β_3)	−5.4**	−4.1**
Constant	3.0**	1.2**

**Statistically significant at the 1% level.
*Statistically significant at the 5% level (one-sided).
Notes: As of 31 December 2015. The recession indicator corresponds to NBER dates shifted forward in time by one quarter (three months) to proxy for the market's tendency to lead macroeconomic developments. Equity returns are excess returns to the Fama–French US market factor. The long-sample regression uses quarterly data from the Federal Reserve's Financial Accounts of the United States; household flows correspond to the change in household equity holdings, net of valuation changes and aggregate issuance, as a percentage of equity market capitalization. The higher-frequency regression uses EPFR Global data on fund flows at a monthly frequency; retail flows correspond to US retail equity fund flows (mutual funds and ETFs) as a percentage of beginning-of-period assets.
Sources: Data library of Kenneth French; EPFR Global; Federal Reserve Statistical Release Z.1, Financial Accounts of the United States; NBER.

Note also the variance ratios for the 5-year/5-year forward Treasury yield. As explained in Chapters 2 and 4, in the past six decades, nominal yields and inflation expectations in the United States have seen two distinct regimes: an increase in the first half of the period and a decrease in the second half. These low-frequency moves tend to dampen the estimated speed of the mean reversion of yields in the history. Treasury yields exhibit stronger reversion properties when an estimate of medium-term expected inflation is subtracted from the nominal yield. This finding is consistent with the notion that real yields are likely to be stationary but inflation expectations need not mean-revert, given the evolving nature of monetary policy over this history.

Whatever its causes, the excess volatility of financial markets has important implications for optimal portfolio construction. As prices cannot diverge from fundamentals without limit, the *excess volatility* of financial markets also suggests *return forecastability*—giving rise to opportunities for value-oriented investors.

Exhibit 5.3. Variance Ratio Estimates of US Equities, US Treasuries, and US Investment-Grade Credit, 1955–2015

	Volatility (% per year)	Variance Ratio (to 1-month variance)					
		3m	6m	1y	2y	3y	5y
US equities, excess returns over cash (1955–2015)							
1955–2015	14.6	1.06	1.16	1.19	1.12	1.03	0.98
1955–1994	14.4	1.04	1.10	1.05	0.79	0.64	0.69
US Treasuries, forward yields (1955–2015)							
5-year × 5-year (changes in yields)	1.11	0.87	0.85	0.91	0.77	0.67	0.74
US investment-grade credit, excess returns over Treasuries (1973–2015)							
Credit (per year of spread duration)	0.53	1.25	1.43	1.40	1.09	0.79	0.54

Notes: As of 31 December 2015. For factor definitions and data sources, see notes to Exhibit 3.1a and the Appendix to Chapter 3 (items A.3.1 and A.3.2).
Sources: Barclays; Bloomberg; Federal Reserve; Gurkaynak, Sack, and Wright (2006); PIMCO.

5.2. Valuation Metrics in Equity Markets

Valuation metrics in equity markets typically involve a comparison of the market capitalization of a firm (or group of firms) to fundamental measures of the firm's earnings or asset base. Some key valuation metrics often used by investors include trailing dividend yield (e.g., past 12-month dividend per share divided by the current price per share), earnings yield, cash flow yield, and the ratio of the book value of the equity of a firm (or group of firms) to its market value. The basic justification for using such valuation ratios (which all have the market value of firms in their denominator) is simply that all such measures should increase if risk premia increase, holding other things constant.[17] As a result, if one were to overweight assets with higher earnings (dividend) yields and underweight those with lower yields,

---

[17]As argued by Wilcox (2007), if we assume that investors' required return on equities is equal to the firm's internal rate of return on retained earnings, we can rewrite the simple dividend discount valuation equation as

$$P = \frac{pE}{r + \lambda - (1 - p)(r + \lambda)} = \frac{E}{(r + \lambda)},$$

where E is the earnings, p is the payout ratio, and r is the return on equity. The expected real total return on equity then equals the earnings yield: $r + \lambda = E/p$.

107

one might be able to capture some of the risk premium that is embedded in these yield differentials.

The use of current earnings or current dividends is subject to the shortcoming that these measures may be too sensitive to business cycle movements. We therefore often use the cyclically adjusted earnings yield (CAEY), defined as the ratio of long-run average earnings to the market capitalization of the firm, as a good indicator of the risk premium. Long-run average earnings—in this case, 10-year average earnings—better represent long-term profitability (see, for example, Campbell and Shiller 1988). Instead of using yields, of course, one can equivalently use price-to-earnings ratios or price-to-dividend ratios, which are simply the inverse of the yields measures mentioned above.

Indicators of valuation can be used in two ways: to position portfolios to be overweight undervalued stocks (or groups of stocks) and underweight overvalued stocks, or to be overweight the market when valuations in the aggregate are cheap and underweight when valuations are expensive. These "cross-sectional" and "time-series" strategies, while related, can have different empirical properties, especially because while the former does not typically have exposures to the market factor, the latter does.

Valuations in the Cross Section. We begin by analyzing a simple cross-sectional valuation strategy implemented across country indices. Consider the performance of a hypothetical investment strategy that chooses which country indices to overweight or underweight based on their earnings yield, dividend yield, and aggregate book-to-market ratios. **Exhibit 5.4** presents a summary of performance statistics of such an investment strategy for the period 1995–2015. These results pertain to a strategy that ranks 10 developed country large-cap equity indices (Australia, Canada, Germany, France, Italy, Japan, Spain, Switzerland, the United Kingdom, and the United States) according to the three valuation ratios mentioned above and groups the top three, middle four, and bottom three countries. The first three columns present the average excess returns (measured in US dollars), the volatility of these returns, and the realized Sharpe ratios of these three groups, and the last column presents the performance of a long–short portfolio of the top three and bottom three countries.

Exhibit 5.4. Performance of a Strategy That Invests in Country-Level Equity Indices, Based on Valuation Metrics, 1995–2015

Valuation Metric	Performance Statistics	Top 3 Countries	Middle 4 Countries	Bottom 3 Countries	Top 3 Minus Bottom 3
Book-to-market ratio					
	Average (% per year)	7.2	6.2	6.8	0.4
	Volatility (% per year)	19.1	18.4	15.5	10.1
	Sharpe ratio	0.37	0.34	0.44	0.04
Earnings yield					
	Average (% per year)	9.6	7.0	3.2	6.5
	Volatility (% per year)	19.3	17.8	16.5	10.4
	Sharpe ratio	0.50	0.40	0.19	0.63
Dividend yield					
	Average (% per year)	7.1	8.3	4.0	3.0
	Volatility (% per year)	19.7	18.6	15.2	11.4
	Sharpe ratio	0.36	0.45	0.27	0.26

Notes: As of 31 December 2015. These computations use monthly excess returns on various country indices from MSCI. Returns are measured in US dollars and are over the US 1-month T-bill rate from Ibbotson Associates. Country-level book-to-market ratios, earnings yields, and dividend yields are aggregated from firm-level data from Compustat.
Sources: Compustat; data library of Kenneth French; MSCI; PIMCO.

Even such simple strategies would have historically realized a positive Sharpe ratio. This experiment suggests that simple valuation metrics could be capturing information about relative risk premia in aggregate equity indices and may be helpful in decisions about which stocks or countries/regions to underweight and overweight in a global equity portfolio. A similar conclusion is obtained by looking at the evidence on the behavior of a cross section of individual stocks classified according to their book-to-market ratios. In **Exhibit 5.5**, we present the performance statistics of the HML portfolio of Fama and French (1992) for their global universe of stocks in 20 countries.

Exhibit 5.5. **Performance of Fama–French Global Portfolios Based on Book-to-Market Ratios, 1990–2015**

Performance Statistics (1990–2015)	Fama–French Global HML Portfolio
Average (% per year)	3.6
Median (% per year)	2.6
Standard deviation (% per year)	7.9
Sharpe ratio (annualized)	0.46

Notes: As of 31 December 2015. Returns data are at monthly frequency.
Sources: Data library of Kenneth French; PIMCO.

Time-Series Strategies: Using Valuations for Timing the Market. We next analyze market-timing strategies based on valuation signals. **Exhibit 5.6** shows the empirical relationship between valuations (as measured by CAEY) and realized excess equity returns. We sort 10-year and 3-year realized excess equity returns from January 1910 to December 2015 on the initial earnings yield. To do so, we divide starting yields into quintiles. Average excess equity returns are closely related to the beginning-of-period percentile rank of CAEY. This link tends to be more powerful at extreme valuations. The sharpest decline in average returns occurs for very low levels of earnings yields, which are consistent with unsustainably high valuations—as were experienced, for example, in the late 1990s during the dot-com bubble. Thus, the cyclically adjusted earnings yield—a remarkably simple measure of valuation—appears to be a reasonable starting point for estimating the current long-term risk premium on equities.

Exhibit 5.6. US Equity Returns (Excess over the Short Rate) as a Function of Starting CAEY, January 1910–December 2015

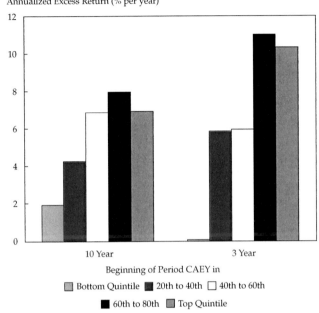

Notes: As of 31 December 2015. Cyclically adjusted earnings yields are taken from Robert Shiller's website. Returns on US equities are at monthly frequency. From June 1926 to December 1954, these are the returns on the equity market factor of Fama and French, taken from the data library of Kenneth French. After this period, they are as defined in the Appendix to Chapter 3 (items A.3.1 and A.3.2). Prior to the start of the Fama–French market factor, equity returns are the returns on the S&P Composite Index, taken from Robert Shiller's website. The short rate is the 1-month US T-bill rate from Ibbotson Associates until December 1954 and is as described in the Appendix to Chapter 3 (items A.3.1 and A.3.2) after this date. Prior to the start of the Fama–French data, the short rate is estimated from annual data reported in the DMS database.

Sources: Data library of Kenneth French; Dimson–Marsh–Staunton (DMS) global database; Ibbotson Associates; Robert Shiller's website; PIMCO.

Caution is warranted, however, in mechanically using valuation metrics like CAEY for near-term positioning. Consider the performance of valuation-based trading strategies that use the information available to the investor at each point in history. **Exhibit 5.7** documents the results of an "active" investment strategy that determines an overlay position in the broad US equity index (over a passive strategy of being fully invested in the index) at the end of each calendar year based on the cyclically adjusted earnings yield. This strategy goes underweight equities when valuations are rich and overweight when valuations are cheap, where the magnitude of the position increases with the richness/cheapness of the valuation metric. In particular, the active position p_t is assumed to be a linear function of the percentile rank q_t of CAEY versus its trailing 10-year history:

$$p_t = 2 * q_t - 1.$$

Thus, the active position held by the investment strategy ranges between −1 and +1. When CAEY is at its median value, the strategy takes no position. Positions are initiated every month and held for 18 months, so the portfolio is composed of 18 trades with overlapping holding periods.

The active investment strategy described above outperformed moderately in the long sample, with a Sharpe ratio of 0.08. However, the Sharpe ratio

Exhibit 5.7. Sharpe Ratios of an Equity Market Timing Strategy Based on CAEY, 1914–2015

	1914–2015			1953–2015		
	Passive	Active	Passive + Active	Passive	Active	Passive + Active
Average excess returns over short-term interest rate (per year)	6.9%	0.9%	7.8%	6.0%	−1.5%	4.5%
Volatility (per year)	17.7%	11.4%	21.1%	14.5%	10.9%	17.2%
Sharpe ratio	0.39	0.08	0.37	0.41	−0.14	0.26
Beta to S&P 500	1.00	0.00	1.00	1.00	−0.07	0.93

Notes: As of 31 December 2015. Returns data are at monthly frequency. Returns on the passive strategy are buy-and-hold excess returns of the US equity market index. The excess return series for the US equity index is as described in the notes to Exhibit 5.6. The statistics reported for the active strategy are for the strategy that goes long or short the US equity market index based on the percentile ranks of the beginning-of-period CAEY. At the beginning of the sample, percentile ranks are computed using an extending window of 3–10 years in length. After 10 years of history is available, percentile ranks are computed using a 10-year rolling window.
Sources: Data library of Kenneth French; Ibbotson Associates; Robert Shiller's website; PIMCO.

of the overall portfolio is lower *with* the overlay than without it, due to the volatility of the active overlay. Worse yet, over the 1950–2015 subsample, the active overlay sustained losses, with a Sharpe ratio of −0.14.

The reason for the relative underperformance of the CAEY-based strategy in the second half of our sample is a persistent decline in the cyclically adjusted earnings yield during the 1990s, which has yet to revert to long-run historical norms, as we show in **Exhibit 5.8**. From the mid-1980s through the early 2000s, CAEY declined to much lower levels than its historical average and stayed there. A valuation-based strategy would therefore have aggressively underweighted equities during most of the bull market of the 1980s and 1990s, experiencing losses. These losses have been only partially recouped because the valuation signal has not reverted to long-run levels over the last 25 years. In other words, an investor using CAEY to time the overall equity market, with only historical information available, would have largely missed out on the windfall from the sustained increase in equity valuations over the last 20 to 30 years.

Uncovering risk premia from valuation metrics is a difficult task and, in a sense, the central challenge of active investing. Valuations are not determined

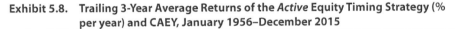

Exhibit 5.8. Trailing 3-Year Average Returns of the *Active* Equity Timing Strategy (% per year) and CAEY, January 1956–December 2015

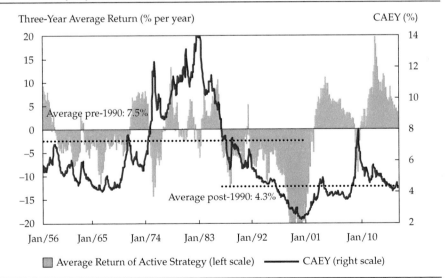

Note: As of 31 December 2015.
Sources: Bloomberg; data library of Kenneth French; Ibbotson Associates; Robert Shiller's website; PIMCO.

by risk premia alone: Expectations of growth in cash flows and the expected path of riskless interest rates also influence valuations. The economic environment can change in a secular manner, altering long-term expectations of growth and the path of interest rates, so the fact that earnings yields or dividend yields are too low relative to history (or a valuation metric based on price-to-earnings ratios or price-to-dividend ratios is too high) may not signal an abnormally low risk premium. Secular movements in the economy can make the time series of valuation metrics such as CAEY extremely persistent, so that the historical record is effectively shorter than it seems. This scenario leads to considerable sampling uncertainty in estimates of the distribution of the valuation metric.[18] The evidence we have documented here demonstrates that a judicious mix of analytical and subjective inputs is required for successful value investing.

5.3. Valuation Metrics for Interest Rates and Credit Spreads

In this section, we analyze valuation signals that anchor interest rates and credit spreads to underlying fundamentals, in a manner similar to using the cyclically adjusted earnings yield to evaluate the attractiveness of the equity market. Encouragingly, we find that the evidence for mean reversion in valuations is somewhat stronger in these markets than in the equity market.

Estimating the Risk Premium in Government Bonds. The determinant of the duration risk premium is how much yields are expected to change relative to what is priced into the yield curve. We can think of the nominal yield to maturity on any riskless zero-coupon bond with maturity τ years, $y(t,\tau)$, as being given by

$$y(t,\tau) = E_t\left(\text{Average nominal policy rate over } [t, t + \tau]\right)$$
$$+ \text{ Interest rate risk premium} + \text{Convexity adjustment}.$$

Typically, the adjustment for convexity explains a small component of variations in bond yields over time. So the key determinant of the interest rate risk premium is one's view on the expected average policy rate over the time to maturity of the bond.

---

[18]Cochrane (2008) demonstrates that even when *all* of the variation in dividend yields is due to variation in expected returns, an investor forecasting returns out of a sample using dividend yields still may do little better than when simply using trailing average returns, due to sampling uncertainty in the relationship between dividend yields and returns.

■ *Carry and roll down of government bonds: Expected returns under a random walk.* The assumption of a random walk in interest rates helps compute a first-cut estimate of expected excess returns on government bonds. This estimate of expected returns, known as "carry," is a commonly used concept in fixed-income markets.

Exhibit 5.9 shows the average shape of the US Treasury yield curve from December 1985 to December 2015. On average, the yield curve is upward sloping in various subsamples. There are two interpretations of an upward-sloping yield curve. The first is that the yield curve simply reflects expectations for higher interest rates in the future. The second is that since interest rate movements are uncertain, a part of the slope of the yield curve is attributable to a premium for bearing interest rate risk (after adjusting for convexity at the long end). More specifically, if riskless yields followed a random walk, the expected excess return on a bond over the horizon to its maturity should be *approximately equal* to the spread between the yield of the bond and the short rate (the "carry" of the bond). Over shorter horizons—such as, say, one year—one also ought to include an estimate of "roll down" (the price return from "rolling down" the yield curve as time to maturity shrinks).

Exhibit 5.9. Average Shape of the US Treasury Yield Curve, 1985–2015

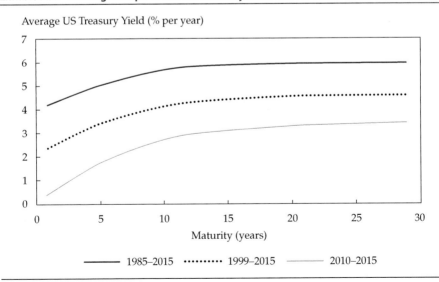

Notes: As of 31 December 2015. Par US Treasury yields are as reported by Gurkaynak, Sack, and Wright (2006).
Sources: Gurkaynak, Sack, and Wright (2006); PIMCO.

The literature finds that, although yields do not quite follow a random walk, yield changes are sufficiently unpredictable to make the slope and carry signals fairly robust quantitative predictors for average excess returns (Fama and Bliss 1987). Predictive regressions (not shown here) of realized 1-year-horizon excess returns to the 10-year Treasury on the beginning-of-period carry have an R^2 in the range of 6%–11%. This compares with an R^2 of around 5% when regressing equity excess returns on CAEY.

Carry-based duration-timing strategies generally have performed well historically, particularly in the cross section, despite this seemingly modest R^2. This result is seen in the performance of a simple investment strategy that overweights and underweights interest rate swaps in different developed countries based on the carry implied in their respective swap curves. In **Exhibit 5.10**, we present a summary of the performance of the following hypothetical strategy trading interest rate swaps in six developed markets (the United States, Germany, Japan, the United Kingdom, Australia, and Canada):

- Rank the six countries in the universe in order of the carry[19] in their swap curve (at the 10-year point) at the beginning of every quarter.

- Receive fixed interest on the 10-year swaps of the top three countries and pay fixed interest on 10-year swaps of the bottom three countries. The duration of each swap in the strategy is set at one year.

Exhibit 5.10. Performance of a Cross-Sectional Duration Strategy Using Interest Rate Swaps, 2002–2015

Sample Period	Performance Statistics	
2002–2015	Average (bps per year)	19
	Standard deviation (bps per year)	52
	Sharpe ratio (annualized)	0.73
2010–2015		
	Average (bps per year)	10
	Standard deviation (bps per year)	42
	Sharpe ratio (annualized)	0.49

Notes: As of 31 December 2015. The carry and excess returns on interest rate swaps of various countries are computed from 10-year (spot and 3-month forward) interest rate swap yields for these countries. Returns data are at quarterly frequency.
Sources: Bloomberg; PIMCO.

---

[19]We define carry as the 12-month forward 10-year swap rate less the spot 10-year swap rate. This definition of carry includes the "roll down" of the swap curve.

It is evident from Exhibit 5.10 that a simple investment strategy of buying duration in high-carry countries and selling it in low-carry markets has generated positive excess returns in our sample. This observation is consistent with the idea that the carry (or, more generally, the slope of the curve) itself contains information about the interest rate premium in various yield curves.

■   *Beyond carry: Macroeconomic conditions and interest rates.*   Although carry provides a reasonable starting point for estimating expected returns, it is helpful to anchor valuations to macroeconomic fundamentals as well. There is a natural link between interest rates and economic growth and inflation. Since the expected path of policy rates is determined by medium-term expectations of real growth and inflation, it is reasonable to postulate that the difference between nominal yields and measures of medium-term expected inflation and real growth information about the risk premium embedded in the yield curve.

To exploit these linkages, we formulate a simple valuation metric for 5-year × 5-year Treasury yield based on the macroeconomic outlook. We focus on this part of the curve because, by construction, it looks beyond the horizon over which rate expectations are linked tightly to central bank policy. Beyond five years, rate expectations ought to be more related to medium-horizon forecasts of macroeconomic variables and long-term anchors of policy rates.

In particular, we specify the following valuation metric:

Value measure = 5-year × 5-year forward yield less expected inflation less expected growth,

where expected inflation and expected real growth are meant to be measured over a medium-term horizon. In our implementation of this metric, expected inflation is estimated as the 10-year trailing average of the year-over-year growth in consumer price index (CPI) while expected real growth is estimated as the 10-year trailing average of year-over-year real GDP growth. The 10-year window is designed to reduce the influence of shorter-term cyclical fluctuations, in a manner similar to the averaging of real earnings in the CAEY measure for equities. **Exhibit 5.11** displays the history of this metric from 1960 to 2015.

This simple metric has been a reasonable signal of excess returns of 5-year forwards on the US Treasury 5-year yield. **Exhibit 5.12** displays average forward-looking returns conditional on the beginning-of-period quintile of the valuation signal. Both 10-year and 3-year returns are increasing in signal "cheapness" (high yields relative to inflation and growth).

Exhibit 5.11.   Time Series of the Valuation Metric for US 5-Year × 5-Year Yield, 1960–2015

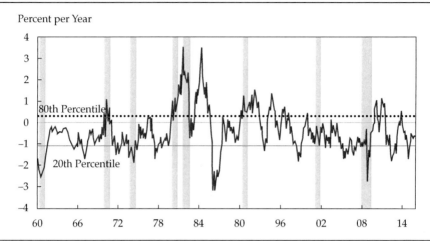

Percent per Year

Notes: As of 31 December 2015. The valuation metric for US 5-year × 5-year yield is computed using (1) 5-year × 5-year yields derived from par US Treasury yields reported by the Federal Reserve (H.15 series) and Gurkaynak, Sack, and Wright (2006) and (2) real GDP growth rates and CPI rates for the United States (from Bloomberg). Shaded periods denote NBER recessions.
Sources: Bloomberg; Federal Reserve; Gurkaynak, Sack, and Wright (2006); PIMCO.

Exhibit 5.12. Average Excess Returns on US 5-Year/5-Year Forwards, Conditional on Beginning-of-Period Valuation Metric, 1960–2015

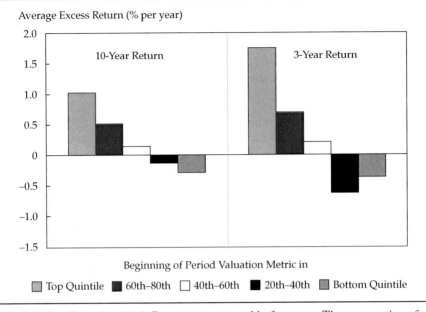

Average Excess Return (% per year)

Notes: As of 31 December 2015. Returns are at monthly frequency. The computation of the returns on US 5-year/5-year forwards is detailed in the Appendix to Chapter 3 (items A.3.1 and A.3.2). The valuation metric for US 5-year × 5-year yield is computed using (1) 5-year × 5-year yields derived from par US Treasury yields reported by the Federal Reserve (H.15 series) and Gurkaynak, Sack, and Wright (2006) and (2) real GDP growth rates and CPI rates for the United States (from Bloomberg).

Sources: Bloomberg; Gurkaynak, Sack, and Wright (2006); PIMCO.

Estimating the Credit Risk Premium. The primary differences between corporate bonds and government bonds are the risk of default, relative illiquidity, and embedded options (e.g., callability). A useful starting point for assessing value in corporate credit is therefore simply the credit spread over government bonds. By adjusting the credit spread for the expected loss from default, we have a simple yet fairly reliable estimate of the expected hold-to-maturity excess returns of corporate bonds over default-free securities.

Exhibit 5.13 shows the history of the default-adjusted credit spread for the Barclays US Credit Index over 1973–2015. To adjust for the expected loss from default, we assume a recovery rate of 40% and use historical default probabilities (1983–2013) conditional on Moody's credit ratings.

As seen in **Exhibit 5.14**, the metric defined above for credit spreads is also associated with prospective returns. As in the case of 5-year × 5-year yields, we see that, on average, a higher value of this metric has been associated with higher prospective returns, supporting the hypothesis that the metric is associated positively with the credit risk premium embedded in credit spreads.

Exhibit 5.13. Default-Adjusted Credit Spread for US Investment-Grade Credit, 1973–2015

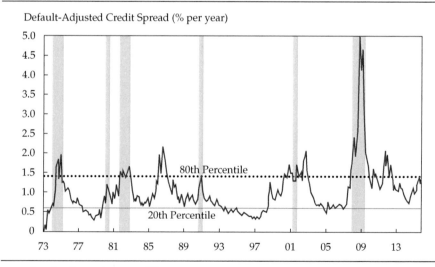

Notes: As of 31 December 2015. The investment-grade credit spread is the published credit spread on the Barclays US Credit Index. The default adjustment is computed using the historical default probabilities for the period 1983–2013 reported by Moody's and the assumption of a recovery rate of 40%. Shaded periods denote NBER recessions.
Sources: Barclays; Bloomberg; Moody's; PIMCO.

Exhibit 5.14. Average Excess Returns on US Investment-Grade Credit, Conditional on Beginning-of-Period Valuation Metric, 1973–2015

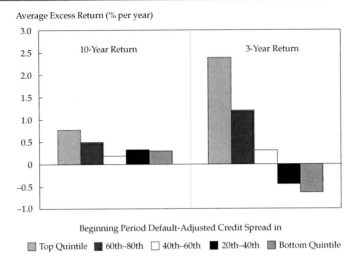

Average Excess Return (% per year)

Beginning Period Default-Adjusted Credit Spread in

□ Top Quintile ■ 60th–80th □ 40th–60th ■ 20th–40th ■ Bottom Quintile

---

Notes: As of 31 December 2015. Returns are at monthly frequency. Excess returns on US investment-grade credit are the published excess returns over duration-matched Treasuries of the Barclays US Credit Index. The valuation metric for US investment-grade credit is computed using the published credit spread for the Barclays US Credit Index and a default adjustment, computed using the historical default probabilities for the period 1983–2013 reported by Moody's and the assumption of a recovery rate of 40%.
Sources: Barclays; Bloomberg; Moody's; PIMCO.

5.4. Testing Valuation Signals in Treasury and Credit Markets

As a further check on these valuation signals in rate and credit markets, we backtest hypothetical investment strategies based on beginning-of-period signals, using the same methodology we employed for the backtest of equity market timing using CAEY. As shown in **Exhibit 5.15**, the 5-year × 5-year strategy realized a Sharpe ratio of 0.35 in the full sample, with positive performance in each of the subsamples we consider (1963–1984 and 1985–2015). Results are reasonable for credit spreads as well, with a full sample (1976–2015) Sharpe ratio of 0.30. Interestingly, the results for both the 5-year × 5-year yields and the investment-grade credit spreads suggest that value-based timing strategies can exhibit positively skewed returns and thereby improve the distributional properties of the overall portfolio. This property of value-oriented strategies can be particularly valuable in improving the properties of returns to credit spread exposures, which tend to be negatively skewed.

Exhibit 5.15. Performance of an Investment Strategy in US 5-Year/5-Year Forwards and US Investment-Grade Credit Based on Their Respective Valuation Metrics (% per year)

	US 5-year x 5-year yield Trailing 10-year Percentile Rank	US Investment Grade Credit Spread Trailing 10-year Percentile Rank
	1963–2015	1976–2015
Average excess return (%, per year)	0.6	0.6
Volatility (%, per year)	1.6	2.0
Sharpe ratio	0.35	0.30
Skew	1.4	1.2
	1963–1984	1976–1984
Average excess return (%, per year)	0.2	0.7
Volatility (%, per year)	1.8	1.3
Sharpe ratio	0.13	0.53
	1985–2015	1985–2015
Average excess return (%, per year)	0.8	0.6
Volatility (%, per year)	1.5	2.2
Sharpe ratio	0.54	0.27

Notes: As of 31 December 2015. Returns are at monthly frequency. Returns on US 5-year/5-year forwards and US investment-grade credit spread returns are as described in the notes to Exhibit 3.1 and the Appendix to Chapter 3 (items A.3.1 and A.3.2). The valuation metric for US 5-year × 5-year yield is computed using (1) 5-year × 5-year yields derived from par US Treasury yields reported by the Federal Reserve (H.15 series) and Gurkaynak, Sack, and Wright (2006) and (2) real GDP growth rates and CPI rates for the United States (from Bloomberg). The valuation metric for US investment-grade credit is computed using the published credit spread for the Barclays US Credit Index and a default adjustment, computed using the historical default probabilities for the period 1983–2013 reported by Moody's and the assumption of a recovery rate of 40%. At the beginning of the sample, percentile ranks are computed using an extending window of 3–10 years in length. After 10 years of history is available, percentile ranks are computed using a 10-year rolling window.

Sources: Barclays; Bloomberg; Federal Reserve; Gurkaynak, Sack, and Wright (2006); Moody's; PIMCO.

5.5. Valuation-Based Investing: Key Takeaways

The basic logic of valuation-based investing is simple: Prices vary inversely with the risk premium, holding everything else constant. Therefore, over-weighting assets whose prices, relative to some measure of their cash flows, are low and underweighting assets whose situation is reversed should capture some of the risk premium differential that may exist between these assets. We have presented evidence across several markets suggesting that valuation-based investing does seem to generate excess returns on average. To the extent that price fluctuations are exaggerated by short-term surges in demand for liquidity, value investing provides liquidity when it is in high demand. Investors with a relatively long-term investment horizon ought to be in a position to engage in such liquidity provision and be compensated for it. Also, to the extent that the logic of value investing is based on earning a risk premium rather than taking advantage of a short-lived market inefficiency, such an investing style is probably sustainable in the long term. It can therefore be argued that the core of a sound investment process should be built around value investing. However, one has to find ways to deal with a few challenges that value investing poses—some of which should be apparent from our discussions in this chapter.

First, prices do not depend on risk premia alone. Variations in prices or yields could also be the result of changes in expectations of cash flows of underlying assets. It is therefore incumbent on value investors to take a nuanced view of expectations over both cyclical and secular horizons. This approach might require investors to blend qualitative and quantitative considerations.

Secondly, no single valuation metric should be used to the exclusion of others. Our empirical experiments suggest that using a "portfolio of signals" approach tends to do a lot better than an approach that relies purely on one signal. Therefore, investors would be well advised to use multiple valuation metrics in their estimation of expected returns and indeed in portfolio construction generally.

Lastly, value-driven investment strategies can see sustained periods of underperformance, given that asset prices tend to mean-revert fairly slowly. This should be clear from the evidence documented in Exhibit 5.8 about the performance of value strategies in US equities in the run-up to the dot-com bust in 2001, and from the experience of bond investors who underweighted the global interest rate markets in recent years. It is therefore often useful to complement valuation-based signals with momentum-driven ones, since the latter conveniently capture high-frequency information embedded in indicators such as fund flows.

6. Putting It All Together: Optimal Portfolio Construction

The objective of active asset allocation should be to construct a portfolio that delivers the highest risk-adjusted returns. In the previous chapters, we have provided a framework for characterizing the expected return and risk of different risk factors. The next step is to synthesize the resulting views into a portfolio.

In a generalized setting, portfolio choice can be viewed as a utility maximization problem for the investor. Typically, investors—be they households saving for retirement (or bequest) or endowments planning to make a stream of payouts—solve a multi-period optimization problem. The assumptions made about the parameterization of the investor's utility function, the stream of consumption the investor is looking to hedge, and the horizon of the investor's optimization problem can all have implications for portfolio choice. While this is an area of interest by itself, we reduce the problem by making a few simplifications.

First, we assume that the investor's risk preferences and liability constraints are embedded in the choice of a benchmark or policy portfolio. For example, an investor who has a highly binding liability constraint would choose a more fixed-income-oriented benchmark, while a working-age individual with a large amount of human capital in his or her "portfolio" would choose an equity-heavy policy portfolio. This assumption allows us to focus our discussion on the choice of an *active overlay* versus this benchmark—thereby simplifying the problem at hand. The optimization problem is effectively one that maximizes the expected returns of the overlay versus the benchmark, subject to the constraint that the *tracking error volatility* of the portfolio (i.e., the standard deviation of the portfolio's excess return over the return of the benchmark) is less than a given limit.

Second, we focus on a one-period optimization problem rather than a multi-period one. This assumption reduces the mathematical complexity of the problem while still offering a realistic reflection of the portfolio construction exercise undertaken by institutional investors, whose performance is often measured over annual horizons.

Third, we assume that the trade-off between expected returns and risk can be quantified in terms of the mean and variance of returns on various risk factors. Thus, in this chapter, we use mean–variance optimization (MVO) as our workhorse model to illustrate issues relating to portfolio construction.

Although portfolio managers in practice do not mechanically construct their portfolios according to any particular optimization program, we show that a simple MVO setup can deliver rich insights into the trade-offs between risk and return.

We begin with a small set of investable factors, without imposing any constraints beyond a cap on portfolio volatility. A couple of important themes emerge from this simple exercise. First, the optimal portfolio favors exposures with high Sharpe ratios while also seeking diversification. As a result, the portfolio may include positive exposures to factors that have relatively unattractive Sharpe ratios if they serve as hedges to other, more attractive factors. This scenario demonstrates the importance of fixed-income investments in diversified portfolios. Second, relative value positions can feature prominently in the optimal portfolio, as the optimization program favors long–short exposures to correlated risk factors with different Sharpe ratios.

We then describe how to determine the main inputs to portfolio construction using a business cycle–oriented approach. We demonstrate the process of blending the slow mean reversion of valuations with a forward-looking view on the state of the macroeconomy to come up with expected returns. Building on the properties of risk factor returns we have described before, we make the case for portfolios to be constructed in a "tail-aware" manner.

The process of macro-aware portfolio construction in an institutional context is then demonstrated using the case of two hypothetical investors: one who has a benign forward-looking view of the US economy and another who has a relatively bearish view. These experiments point out the key considerations in portfolio choice, as well as offering some practical insights into the robustness of the conclusions of such an exercise.

6.1. Key Trade-Offs in Portfolio Construction: A Simple Example

To illustrate the main trade-offs in a typical portfolio construction problem, we begin with a simple example. We consider the problem of an investor who seeks an optimal portfolio over a tactical horizon (say, 12 months) and measures performance relative to a benchmark. The investor's objective is to choose an overlay to maximize expected excess return over the benchmark subject to the constraint that the *tracking error volatility* of the portfolio (i.e., the standard deviation of the portfolio's excess return over the return of the benchmark) is less than a given limit. A formal description of the optimization program and the optimal solution is provided in the Appendix (A.6.1).

Suppose that the benchmark of the investor consists of US Treasuries, US equities, and US corporate bonds. The factors to which risk can be allocated are (1) US Treasury yields (represented by the 5-year Treasury yield factor), (2) the US equity market index return (represented by the return on the S&P 500 Index), and (3) corporate spreads (represented by the returns on the Barclays US investment-grade corporate bond index, hedged with US Treasuries to neutralize its duration risk). Suppose that the investor is subject to a tracking error volatility constraint of 100 bps per year.[20]

Exhibit 6.1 displays the Sharpe ratios assumed for the risk factors in this example. These Sharpe ratios are illustrative. Under these assumptions, credit offers the most attractive risk-adjusted return, followed by equities, and finally by government debt.

Exhibit 6.1. Sharpe Ratios of Risk Factors in the Opportunity Set

	Sharpe Ratio
5-Year US Treasuries	0.1
S&P 500	0.2
Corporate spreads	0.4

Note: Hypothetical example, for illustration only.
Sources: PIMCO.

For correlations, we start from the simple, but not particularly realistic, assumption that every risk factor has a mildly positive correlation with every other factor. We proceed to iteratively alter our correlation assumptions to be more consistent with historical experience, and we document how these changes affect the MVO allocation. **Exhibit 6.2** shows the upper triangle of the three correlation matrices employed in this exercise.

Exhibit 6.3 displays the optimal overlays in various cases. The first column (Case 1) shows the results for the case in which all assets are symmetrically positively correlated with one another. As expected, the investment offering the most attractive risk-adjusted expected return—duration-hedged corporate bonds—receives the largest allocation of 90 bps of standalone volatility exposure. Standalone volatility exposure allocated to a risk factor is defined as the product of the allocated exposure to a risk factor

---

[20]The particular risk limit is not important in this simple setting, because the optimal portfolio scales with the volatility target.

Exhibit 6.2. Correlation Assumptions across Various Assets Used for Optimization

	Case 1		Case 2		Case 3	
	S&P 500	Corporate Spreads	S&P 500	Corporate Spreads	S&P 500	Corporate Spreads
Treasuries	20%	20%	**−15%**	**−35%**	−15%	−35%
S&P 500	—	20%	—	20%	—	**62%**

Note: Hypothetical example, for illustration only.
Source: PIMCO.

Exhibit 6.3. Mean–Variance-Optimal Overlays for a 100 bps Tracking Error Budget: Sensitivity to Assumed Factor Correlations

	Case 1	Case 2	Case 3
Optimal allocation			
US 5-Year Treasuries (years of duration)	0 yrs	0.7 yr	0.7 yr
S&P 500 (% overweight)	2.0%	2.0%	−1.5%
Corporate spreads (years of spread duration)	1.8 yrs	1.9 yrs	2.4 yrs
Standalone volatility of exposures (in basis points)			
US Treasuries	0	58	59
S&P 500	30	30	−22
Corporate spreads	90	95	117
Contribution to portfolio risk (basis points)[A]	100 (total)	100 (total)	100 (total)
US Treasuries	0	12	12
S&P 500	14	12	−9
Corporate spreads	86	76	97
Portfolio Sharpe ratio	0.42	0.50	0.48

Note: Hypothetical example, for illustration only.
[A]The contribution to portfolio volatility of an exposure $w(i)$ to factor i is defined as
$$\frac{\partial \sigma(w)}{\partial w(i)} w(i) = \left(w^T \Sigma_R \right)_i w(i) / \sigma(w),$$
where w corresponds to the $K \times 1$ vector of portfolio positions, Σ_R is the $K \times K$ covariance matrix, and $\sigma(w)$ is the volatility of the portfolio. This measure has the attractive property that all volatility contributions add up to the total portfolio volatility; that is,
$$\sum_{i=1}^{K} \frac{\partial \sigma(w)}{\partial w(i)} w(i) = \sigma(w).$$

Sources: PIMCO; Bloomberg; Barclays.

and the standard deviation of the factor return.[21] Stated in terms of spread duration, the optimal overlay calls for adding 1.8 years of spread duration relative to the benchmark. This allocation contributes 86 bps of the total available risk budget of 100 bps per year. At the same time, the portfolio diversifies by holding some equities as well (an overweight of 2%), despite their inferior risk-adjusted expected return. The optimal allocation to government bonds is zero, as the expected return and diversification benefit of government bonds are offset by the opportunity cost of smaller allocations to equities and to credit.

Next, in Case 2, we alter the correlations to reflect the fact that government bonds are negatively correlated with equities and credit spreads, consistent with their behavior over the last 20 years. Under these assumptions, the mean–variance-optimal portfolio assigns a substantial positive allocation to government bonds, even though their expected return (per unit of volatility) is still quite modest. Due to the negative correlation of Treasury returns with equity and credit returns, the contribution of the Treasury position to portfolio volatility (12 bps) is lower than its standalone volatility (58 bps). This correlation permits the portfolio to hold more credit spread exposures and more Treasuries while remaining within the volatility budget. As a result, the Sharpe ratio for the optimal portfolio improves from 0.42 to 0.50.

Finally, in Case 3, we use a larger, positive correlation between credit spreads and equities of 62%, which is comparable to their historical correlation over the last 20 years. Now the mean–variance-optimal portfolio underweights equities (the standalone volatility exposure to this investment is negative), despite their positive Sharpe ratio. Underweighting equities permits a larger allocation to the relatively attractive credit investment. Put another way, the gap between the Sharpe ratios of these reasonably highly correlated assets is sufficiently large that holding a long–short position is optimal. Also, because positive Sharpe ratio positions in the opportunity set now have a more positive correlation, the Sharpe ratio for the optimal portfolio declines marginally from 0.50 to 0.48.

These simple cases highlight important considerations in portfolio construction. First, some assets, such as government bonds, hedge portfolio returns in recessions. As we show in Case 2 (Exhibit 6.3), an optimally constructed portfolio would hold positive exposures to government bonds even if their Sharpe ratios were relatively poor. This case demonstrates the central role that fixed-income investments play in diversified portfolios, especially when investors seek to limit losses in "left-tail" events. Second, risk exposures to "relative value" positions appear frequently in unconstrained optimizations,

---

[21]See the Appendix (item A.6.1) for a fuller description.

as we see in the comparison of Cases 2 and 3. These relative value views tend to emerge from differences between the Sharpe ratios of correlated assets. These views ought to be stress-tested because the optimization program would likely capitalize on small presumed differences in expected returns across correlated risk factors. The possible antidotes to this problem are to examine the return assumptions carefully and to constrain the size of relative value positions, if necessary.

6.2. Portfolio Construction in a Macro-Oriented Setting: Main Ingredients

We now turn to the more realistic tactical asset allocation problem of a global multi-asset investor. A business cycle–oriented approach has natural applications in this context. The key inputs to this asset allocation problem—forecasts of expected returns of factors—are intimately related to views on the state of the macroeconomy. We demonstrate that the use of a macro-oriented approach generates a nuanced set of forward-looking inputs and therefore a more soundly constructed portfolio.

Estimating Expected Returns and Sharpe Ratios. We illustrate the process of arriving at a forecast of expected returns in the case of US equities. Forming a view on equities is fundamental to one's assessment of other risk factors, such as corporate credit. Additionally, the US equity market offers a rich dataset of historical returns and valuations over several business cycles, which is essential for calibrating the parameters required to compute expected returns and risk. The principles we describe here are applicable to other risk factors as well.

Defining a Tractable Value Metric. The first step in estimating *ex ante* Sharpe ratios is to select an analytically tractable valuation metric. For the US equity market factor, we take this metric to be cyclically adjusted earnings yield (CAEY), which is the inverse of the cyclically adjusted price-to-earnings multiple. As discussed before, this valuation metric compares prices to a trailing 10-year average of earnings, thereby smoothing out cyclical variations. In general, we prefer earnings yield to its inverse, since it is more robust at the extremes of earnings: As earnings fall towards zero, the price-to-earnings multiple increases non-linearly, while the earnings yield declines more gradually. **Exhibit 6.4** presents the time series of CAEY.

As we discussed in Chapter 5, equity valuation metrics such as the CAEY mean-revert over 3- to 5-year horizons. The mean to which they revert, however, has not been constant over time. The slow-moving secular variations in this valuation metric are clear from Exhibit 6.4. Earnings yields rose sharply

Exhibit 6.4. Historical Estimates of Cyclically Adjusted Earnings Yields of US Equities, 1950–2015

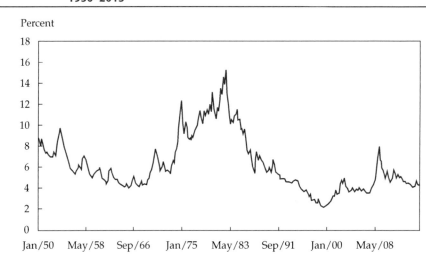

Percent

Jan/50   May/58   Sep/66   Jan/75   May/83   Sep/91   Jan/00   May/08

Notes: As of 31 December 2015. Assumptions used for historical estimates of the equity risk premium (ERP) are as follows: Cyclically adjusted dividend yield is the product of the CAEY and the median dividend payout ratio since 1950 (estimated at 50%); real rate is the 10-year TIPS (Treasury Inflation-Protected Securities) yield (nominal rates less average trailing inflation before 1998); growth is the trailing 10-year average of real GDP growth less average population growth since 1950 (1.2% per year until 2004, declining secularly to 1.0% per year currently).
Sources: Bloomberg; Robert Shiller's website; PIMCO.

in the first half of the sample and have declined equally sharply since the early 1980s. Even a simple model of equity valuations, such as the Gordon and Shapiro (1956) growth model, would tell us that the level of real interest rates can have a significant bearing on earnings yields. Indeed, real interest rates rose sharply in the late 1970s, during the period of the Volcker Federal Reserve, and have declined steadily since the early 1980s.

Some of the decline in earnings yields since the early 1980s can be attributed to the secular decline in real interest rates. We therefore define the equity risk premium (ERP) as

$$ERP \equiv CAEY \times \text{Payout ratio} + E\left(\text{Real earnings growth}\right)$$
$$- E\left(\text{Real interest rate}\right).$$

The first term is an estimate of "cyclically adjusted" dividend yields to shareholders, which should include cash returned via both dividends and share buybacks. The second term incorporates the expectation of growth into these cash flows. The last term adjusts for the effect of interest rates in pricing the present value of cash flows.

In **Exhibit 6.5,** we present the history of our estimate of the ERP since 1950. Despite having adjusted for the effect of interest rates, we find that the estimate of ERP has declined systematically over the past 65 years. The decline has often been attributed to one-off effects, such as advances in technology that have improved liquidity and the efficacy of arbitrage capital in US equity markets—a view that would prompt us to believe that average ERP going forward will be closer to recent experience. On the other hand, the post-1980s period (until the financial crisis of 2008) was also one of extraordinary calm in the macroeconomy and financial markets, which might not recur. This view would prompt us to believe that the average ERP going forward will be higher than it has been since the mid-1980s. Given these competing arguments, we use the unconditional average since 1950 of 3.1% as the mean to which ERP is likely to revert over the next three to five years.

Exhibit 6.5. Historical Estimates of ERP, 1950–2015

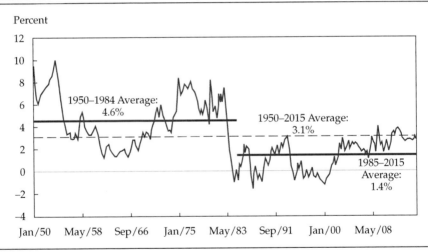

Note: As of 31 December 2015.
Sources: Bloomberg; Robert Shiller's website; PIMCO.

Systematic Variations in the Valuation Metric over the Business Cycle. We now turn to estimating variations in equity valuations over the business cycle. **Exhibit 6.6** presents averages of ERP in recessions and expansions (according to NBER dates) since 1950. To adjust for the secular decline seen in ERP in the history, we also examine averages of ERP *relative to* its trend (defined as a trailing 3-year average). The negative average trend-adjusted ERP over the past 65 years is a direct consequence of the secular decline. On average, ERP was higher than its trend by 0.8% in recessions and lower than its trend by 0.2% in expansions, coinciding with the underperformance of equities in recessions and their outperformance, on average, in expansions.

Using deviations from trend as our guide to cyclical variations in ERP, rather than its level, allows us to conveniently account for our forward-looking views on the long-term average of equity valuations. We alter the distribution of these deviations slightly to be consistent with the view that ERP averages going forward are likely to be the same as the average over the past 65 years (i.e., the secular decline in ERP will not continue in the future and the average deviation from trend would be zero rather than negative). The variations of the metric around this "re-centered" mean are preserved in our calculations to be consistent with historical experience.

Exhibit 6.6. Historical Estimates of ERP over the Business Cycle, 1950–2015

1950–2015	Unconditional Average	Average in Recessions	Average in Expansions
ERP	3.1%	4.7%	2.8%
ERP vs. trailing 3-year average	−0.1	0.8	−0.2
ERP vs. trend: forward-looking view	0	0.76	−0.13

Note: As of 31 December 2015.
Sources: Bloomberg; Robert Shiller's website; PIMCO.

Estimating Expected Return on Equities Given a View on the State of the Economy. The empirical properties of ERP that we have documented above help us forecast expected returns on US equities, say, over a one-year horizon, given a view on the macroeconomy. Consider two hypothetical investors as of the end of December 2015. The first investor views the probability of a recession in the US economy over a one-year horizon to be 15%. This figure equals the fraction of time that the US economy has spent in recessions in the last 50 years. The second investor has a particularly bearish view on the state of the US economy and believes that the probability of recession is 50% over a one-year horizon.

In **Exhibit 6.7**, we present the calculation of *ex ante* expected returns of US equities over cash from the perspectives of the two investors. We begin by estimating the ERP as of 31 December 2015. Given a cyclically adjusted P/E multiple of 22.6 and a dividend payout expectation of 55% of earnings, the cyclically adjusted dividend yield is 2.45%. Assuming that expected real growth of earnings will outstrip the real interest rate by 0.5%, we estimate the ERP to be 2.95%—which is only 0.15% below its mean of 3.1%. If this deviation from fair value is reduced by 50% over a 3-year period, the annual expected price return in real terms would be modest at approximately −0.8%, before accounting for any business cycle–related variations in equity valuations.

Since the first investor forecasts the probability of recession to be equal to the unconditional probability, the contribution of the cyclical effect to expected changes in valuations is equal to zero. The expected real price decline therefore remains at 0.8%. When combined with an expected near-term dividend yield of 3.1% (assumed equal to the 12-month trailing dividend yield), expected inflation of 1.8%, and a funding cost of 0.6% (equal to the 1-year US Treasury yield), the result is an expected excess return over cash of 3.5%.

Exhibit 6.7. Estimating *Ex Ante* Sharpe Ratio for US Equities (S&P 500), as of 31 December 2015

	Case 1: 15% Recession Probability	Case 2: 50% Recession Probability
ERP as of 31 Dec 2015	2.95%	2.95%
Expected ERP in 1 year	2.98%	3.25%
Expected 12-month dividend yield (1)	3.1%	3.1%
Expected real price return (2)	−0.8%	−11.7%
Expected inflation (3)	1.8%	1.4%
Expected nominal total return (1) + (2) + (3)	4.1%	−7.3%
Expected excess return over cash	3.5%	−7.9%
Sharpe ratio	0.24	−0.46

Notes: As of 31 December 2015. Hypothetical example, for illustrative purposes only. Assumptions for ERP forecasts are as follows: Payout ratio is taken to be 55% currently to account for higher buyback yield than historically observed; expected real earnings growth is taken to be 0.75% per year (expected GDP growth of 1.75% per year less population growth of 1% per year); expected real interest rate is taken to be 0.25% per year.

Source: PIMCO. Hypothetical example. For illustration only.

In the case of the second investor, who estimates a 50% probability of recession, the forecast change in the ERP would be 0.3% (0.5 × 0.76% − 0.5 × 0.13%). This result, in addition to the slow drift up in ERP due to mean reversion, would lead to a forecast of a sharp correction in equities—of approximately −11.7% over a 1-year period. This scenario results in a significantly lower estimate of expected excess return, −7.9%.

As shown in Chapter 3, the volatility of risk factor returns also varies systematically over the business cycle. The portfolio optimization exercise that is anchored in a view on the business cycle should therefore also incorporate such variations. We compute a forecast of equity return volatility based on the conditional volatilities of US equity returns shown in Exhibit 3.3 and the variance of conditional expectations of equity returns implied by the changes in ERP in recessions and expansions shown in Exhibit 6.3. Our forecast of equity return volatility in Case 1 comes out to 14.5% per year, close to the unconditional long-sample volatility estimate for US equity returns. In Case 2, where the outlook for the US economy is grimmer, the forecast of equity return volatility is higher, at 17.2% per year.

The estimates of forecast Sharpe ratios for US equities therefore come to 0.24 in the case of the first investor and −0.46 in the case of the second investor. This example demonstrates the importance of taking a view on the business cycle in arriving at expected return forecasts. Despite having identical models of valuations and identical long-horizon views on equities, the two investors end up with dramatically different tactical forecasts of expected returns.

Expected Returns of Other Risk Factors. Expected returns of other key risk factors are estimated along similar lines. The results are presented in **Exhibit 6.8**, which shows a scatterplot of *ex ante* Sharpe ratio estimates made by the two hypothetical investors.

Risk factors that lie on the 45-degree line are those that exhibit no sensitivity of valuations to the business cycle. The farther a risk factor lies from this 45-degree line, the more sensitive its valuations are to the outlook for the macroeconomy. Factors that underperform in relatively weak economic conditions ("procyclical factors," such as global equities, corporate credit spreads, and EM currencies) fall below the 45-degree line, while those that outperform in periods of weakness (e.g., developed market government bonds and JPY/USD) fall above it. The dispersion of *ex ante* Sharpe ratios around the 45-degree line demonstrates the importance of the business cycle in determining one's views on risk factors—and hence on optimal portfolio positioning.

Exhibit 6.8. Sharpe Ratios of Key Risk Factors: 15% vs. 50% Probability of Recession over a 1-Year Horizon

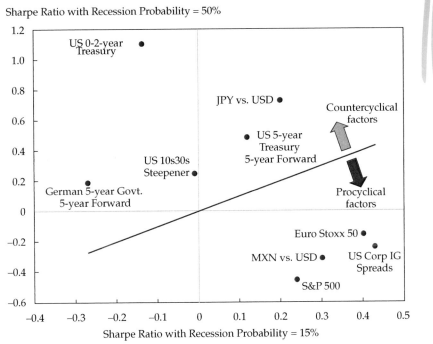

Notes: As of 31 December 2015. Hypothetical example, for illustrative purposes only.
Source: PIMCO.

6.3. Practical Considerations in Portfolio Construction: Imposing Constraints

The portfolio optimization problem described in section 6.1 is useful for building an understanding of the main trade-offs involved in portfolio construction. However, in a practical setting, several constraints need to be imposed on the process in order to obtain actionable outcomes. We describe three key practical considerations that ought to be embedded as constraints in the portfolio construction problem.

Incorporating Tail Awareness into Portfolio Choice. The first—and perhaps the most economically meaningful—consideration is the need to limit losses in a "left-tail" event. This consideration often arises in an institutional context—particularly in the case of active overlays on fixed-income benchmarks. Investors who allocate assets to be actively managed against fixed-income benchmarks do so with the view that these allocations should serve as sources of liquidity in periods of economic stress. When an active fixed-income overlay is tilted heavily towards negatively skewed risk factors, its efficacy as a source of liquidity becomes severely impeded.

More generally, controlling the left tail of the distribution of portfolio returns is necessary if the opportunity set includes risk factors with embedded negative convexity. Comparing a diversified portfolio of equities and a diversified portfolio of credit-risky bonds, we would typically find that the downside skew of the spread returns on the credit portfolio is worse than that of the equity portfolio (after normalizing by volatility differences), especially if the credit portfolio consisted of investment-grade credits. We illustrated this property of credit returns in Chapter 3, where we presented evidence that credit excess returns have a significantly higher beta to equities on the downside than they do on the upside. In the absence of explicit constraints, it is possible for optimization programs to substitute exposure to credit spreads for exposure to equities, thereby leading to portfolios that perform worse in particularly weak states of the macroeconomy.

A word of caution is in order, however, about bringing left-tail considerations into portfolio choice. Sometimes, practitioners tend to push the issue of controlling losses in left-tail events too far, recasting the portfolio choice problem as a trade-off directly between expected returns and forecasts of losses in periods of stress, often defined as conditional expectations of returns in the bottom 5%–10% of the distribution (CVaR, or "conditional value at risk"). While this "Mean vs. CVaR" approach could be appropriate for a portfolio of particularly convex assets, such as out-of-the-money options, in our view, it is not ideal for a top-down asset allocation exercise whose opportunity set is dominated by modestly skewed risk factors. The degree of estimation error is significantly larger when one focuses on a small part of the returns distribution of risk factors rather than its entirety. Our preferred formulation of the problem is as a trade-off between mean and variance, while including *tail awareness* through an additional constraint that expected losses in the "left tail" (bottom 5%–10% of the distribution) be no larger than a predetermined limit.

To calibrate expected returns of various risk factors in a left-tail event, we examine their performance during historical periods of market stress. Generally speaking, such periods are characterized by large drawdowns in equities, credit spreads, and emerging market assets and substantial outperformance of developed market government bonds and certain risk-off currencies, such as JPY/USD. To capture the effects of a left-tail event, we start with an estimate of the first principal component of a broad range of risk factor returns. This turns out to load positively on procyclical factors, like equities and credit spreads, and negatively on countercyclical ones, like developed market government bonds and JPY/USD. The expected return of any risk factor in a left-tail event is defined to be the historical average return on the risk factor in periods in which the rolling 6-month returns of the first principal component is in the bottom 5% of its empirical distribution.

Estimates of the left-tail risk of a selection of factors are shown in **Exhibit 6.9.** As expected, we find credit spreads to have higher left-tail risk ($-2.6 \times$ volatility) than equities ($-2.0 \times$ volatility), and higher than if these returns were normally distributed. A constraint that limits expected portfolio returns in the left tail would therefore curtail exposures to credit spreads, unless the incremental benefit to expected portfolio returns were enough to compensate for the greater risk.

Exhibit 6.9. Left-Tail Properties and Correlation with US Equities: Select Risk Factors

	Correlation with S&P 500	Expected Return in 5% Left-Tail Scenario (# of standard deviations)
Duration		
US Treasuries 0–2 years	−35%	0.9
US 5-year/5-year forward	−7%	1.6
US 10- to 30-year steepener	−26%	1.0
German 5-year/5-year forward	6%	1.0
US Investment Grade Corporate Credit spreads	65%	−2.6
Equities		
S&P 500	100%	−2.0
EURO STOXX 50	70%	−2.0
Currencies		
Long JPY/USD	−15%	1.0
Long MXN/USD	49%	−1.3

Notes: As of 31 December 2015.
Sources: Bloomberg; PIMCO.

Constraints on Relative Value Positions. Even in the simple three-asset problem presented in section 6.1, we saw that the optimal portfolio allocated risk to a long credit versus equity relative value trade. This outcome arose as a consequence of the gap between the Sharpe ratios of credit and equities, which were assumed to be highly correlated with each other. Highly correlated assets should, in principle, have similar Sharpe ratios because a high correlation tells us that the assets are exposed to a common set of systematic risk factors.

Often, such inconsistencies between inputs are unintended and caused by estimation errors. An unconstrained mean–variance optimization problem may end up maximizing the effects of such errors. In our view, the criticism of MVOs as "error maximizers" is not an insurmountable one. The solution to this issue lies in being careful to control the amount of risk allocated to such relative value positions.

Investors often have active views on the relative valuations of correlated risk factors. For example, both the hypothetical investors considered in Exhibit 6.8 would have had the view in December 2015 that the expected returns of corporate credit spreads were more attractive than those of equities. Consequently, their portfolios would have ended up being overweight credit relative to equities. However, these investors ought to be careful to measure the risk allocated to this relative value position and examine whether the exposure is consistent with their conviction in the expected return differential. It is often useful to stress test the assumptions behind such large differences in forecasts of expected returns—and assess whether these assumptions are robust to varying sets of parameter inputs and qualitative views.

The easiest way to control relative value positions is to constrain the risk allocated to each relative value position. In the presence of such a constraint, the solution to the problem would by definition be consistent with the investor's *ex ante* conviction in the position—that is, the investor's assessment of his or her skill in determining the attractiveness of a given relative value position.

Institutional Constraints on Portfolio Allocation. Constraints on portfolio allocation can also relate to investment mandates. The most common is a constraint that prohibits portfolio managers from selling securities short. Similarly, investment mandates might disallow holding securities if they fall below a certain credit quality (often defined in terms of ratings). Institutional mandates might also disallow excessive leverage in portfolios. Leverage is often employed by portfolio managers to gain exposures to certain risk factors (such as a duration-neutral steepener trade). However, such exposures can be fraught with a significant degree of risk in scenarios of stress, often because of the inability to refinance positions—a vulnerability that warrants limits on the amount of leverage allowed. In order for portfolio managers to abide by such rules, constraints might have to be imposed on the size of allowable positions.

6.4.   Optimal Portfolio Construction: A Case Study

We now present a case study that demonstrates the principles of portfolio construction that we have discussed above. We return to the two hypothetical investors seen in section 6.2, who have the same valuation framework but differ in their views on the US economy over a 1-year horizon.

Case 1. Probability of a recession in the United States over a 1-year horizon of 15%

Case 2. Recession probability over a 1-year horizon of 50% (a stress case)

In each case, we solve for a portfolio that has a tracking error volatility budget of 200 bps versus its benchmark, with the constraint that expected losses in a left-tail scenario do not exceed 400 bps. The correlation and volatility estimates that we use in the following experiments are combinations of estimates from a long sample and from a recent sample of the time series of factor returns. This approach helps address the concern that changes in the macroeconomic regime can lead to shifts in correlations that may not be adequately captured if one were to equally weight all historical observations. At the same time, the estimates are not completely governed by recent experience.

Properties of the Optimal Portfolio in Case 1   Let us first consider the optimal allocation in Case 1, which embeds a relatively benign forward-looking view of the US economy (see **Exhibit 6.10**). The optimal allocation has an overall "risk-on" tilt and an equity beta of 8.2%. This risk-on tilt arises largely from the overweight position in US corporate IG spreads. In fact, as shown in **Exhibit 6.11**, most of the risk of this portfolio comes from the three years of spread duration overweight in US corporate IG spreads.

However, this spread duration overweight is balanced by the inclusion of a few risk-off positions—namely, an underweight in the S&P 500, an overweight in duration in the intermediate part of the US yield curve (via the exposure to the US 5-year × 5-year yield), and an overweight in JPY/USD. The optimal portfolio balances risk-on and risk-off exposures, particularly because of the constraint limiting losses in a left-tail event.

While the portfolio is designed to limit expected losses in left-tail events, there are two elements of its construction that warrant a closer look. First,

139

Exhibit 6.10. Mean–Variance-Optimal Portfolio: Tracking Error Volatility of 200 bps per Year

	Case 1: Recession Probability = 15%
Beta of duration positions to US Treasuries	0.5
US Treasuries 0–2 years (years of duration)	−0.4
US Treasury 5-year/5-year forward (years of duration)	0.9
US 10- to 30-year steepener (years of duration per leg)	0.4
German Government 5-year/5-year forward (years of duration)	−1.0
US corp IG spreads (years of spread duration)	3.0
Equities (% allocation)	−0.1%
S&P 500	−4.7%
EURO STOXX 50	4.6%
Currencies (% allocation)	−5.6%
Long JPY/USD	4.5%
Long MXN/USD	1.1%

Note: Hypothetical example, for illustration only.
Sources: Barclays; Bloomberg; PIMCO.

Exhibit 6.11a. Mean–Variance-Optimal Portfolio: Risk Detail

	Case 1: Recession Probability = 15%
Equity beta	8.2%
Expected return in left-tail scenario	−400 bps

Note: Hypothetical example, for illustration only.
Sources: Barclays; Bloomberg; PIMCO.

Exhibit 6.11b.   Mean–Variance-Optimal Portfolio: Risk Detail

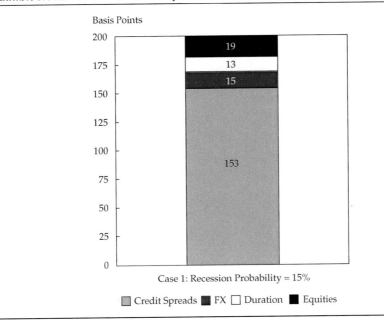

Basis Points

Case 1: Recession Probability = 15%

■ Credit Spreads ■ FX □ Duration ■ Equities

its risk is dominated by the overweight position in US corporate investment-grade spreads: Roughly 150 bps out of the 200 bp tracking error volatility budget is devoted to this trade. Such a large concentration of risk in a single position ought to be examined carefully, since it indicates a lack of diversification in the portfolio. However, in this particular instance, this concentrated position reflects the fact that at the time of performing this exercise, corporate credit was indeed deemed to be the most attractively valued factor in the opportunity set. In some measure, it also reflects the stylized nature of the experiment, in which only a few, admittedly highly correlated risk factors have been included in the opportunity set. The inclusion of macro and bottom-up relative value positions would have automatically reduced the risk allocation to corporate credit.

Second, as expected, the portfolio embeds some implicit relative value views. For example, the positions imply a view that US equities are likely to underperform European equities and that US duration will outperform European duration. In its quest to reduce portfolio risk from market exposures on the margin, MVO brings in some relative value views. Both of these relative value views originate from the thesis that there will be a convergence in the medium-term growth outlook of the US and European economies, leading to an outperformance of European equities and US duration.

Portfolio Allocation with a Bearish View on the Economy. Let us now compare this portfolio allocation with the one in Case 2, in which the second hypothetical investor has a fairly bearish view on the economy. Given this view, most risk-on factors, such as equities and corporate credit, have negative expected returns, while US intermediate duration is markedly more attractive than it is in Case 1. We present a comparison of the optimal positioning in the two cases in **Exhibit 6.12**.

Optimal portfolio allocations largely reflect this configuration of Sharpe ratios. As shown in Exhibit 6.12, the allocation in Case 2 has materially higher exposure to US duration. The exposure to the front end of the US yield curve flips from being negative in Case 1 to being positive in Case 2. This difference is largely an effect of the view that in a recession, central banks would have to consider extraordinary easing measures, such as potentially allowing short rates to be negative.

The allocation to equities turns negative in Case 2 (as opposed to the neutral equity positioning in Case 1). However, even in this relatively bearish case for the US economy, we find that the optimal positioning in US corporate credit spreads is a small overweight. The relative overweight positioning in credit versus equity is preserved in Case 2 as well (in terms of direction—the magnitude of the exposure is arguably different in the two cases). This positioning reflects a view of relatively attractive valuations of credit spreads. In fact, the credit spread versus equity positioning in Case 2 serves to increase the conviction in the allocations in Case 1. An investor who has a relatively benign view on the US economy could look at Case 2 as a "stress test" of his or her assumptions—and would find confirmation of the conclusion that overweight credit spreads would be a robust trade.

The optimal allocation to MXN/USD is a good counterexample. While the portfolio in Case 1 has a modest overweight (1.1%) to MXN, this position does not appear in the optimal allocation in Case 2. This result shows that the position in MXN was less robust than the credit versus equity position. It is often useful to examine portfolio positioning under alternate macro views, as a way to tease out the robustness of recommendations for portfolio positioning.

Exhibit 6.12. **Optimal Portfolio for Benign vs. Bearish Outlook on the US Economy: Tracking Error Volatility of 200 bps per Year**

	Case 1: Recession Probability = 15%	Case 2: Recession Probability = 50%
Beta of duration positions to US Treasuries	0.5	1.7
US Treasuries 0–2 years (years of duration)	−0.4	0.5
US Treasury 5-year × 5-year (years of duration)	0.9	1.5
US 10- to 30-year steepener (years of duration per leg)	0.4	−0.6
German Government 5-year × 5-yearr (years of duration)	−1.0	0.1
US corp IG spreads (years of spread duration)	3.0	0.3
Total equity (% allocation)	−0.1%	−5.0%
S&P 500	−4.7%	−7.7%
EURO STOXX 50	4.6%	2.7%
FX (% allocation)	−5.6%	−4.7%
Long JPY/USD	4.5%	4.7%
Long MXN/USD	1.1%	0.0%

Note: Hypothetical example, for illustration only.
Sources: Barclays; Bloomberg; PIMCO.

Exhibit 6.13 shows additional details of the risk characteristics of the two optimal portfolios. The portfolio in Case 2 has a negative equity beta (−6.7%) and in fact is expected to outperform in a left-tail outcome for the macroeconomy. This result is unsurprising given the overweight to duration and underweight to equities. The risk of the portfolio is dominated by duration risk: Roughly 130 bps out of the 200 bps of tracking error come from this risk-off tilt. The overweight in credit spreads acts as a diversifier in Case 2, with a negative contribution to portfolio volatility.

Exhibit 6.13a. Risk Detail of Optimal Positioning in Benign vs. Bearish Outlook for the US Economy

	Case 1: Recession Probability = 15%	Case 2: Recession Probability = 50%
Equity beta	8.2%	−6.7%
Expected return in left-tail scenario	−400 bps	360 bps

Note: Hypothetical example, for illustration only.
Sources: Barclays; Bloomberg; PIMCO.

Exhibit 6.13b. Risk Detail of Optimal Positioning in Benign vs. Bearish Outlook for the US Economy

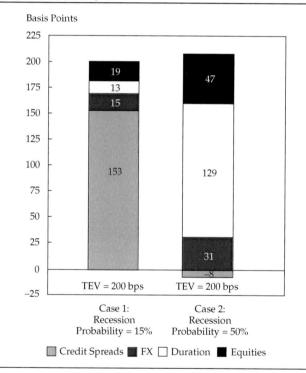

6.5. Conclusion

The basic idea of MVO is simple: Find the allocation that maximizes expected return for a given portfolio volatility. However, despite having been available as a portfolio construction methodology for several decades now, and despite there being a multitude of so-called commercial "optimization tools" that employ the mean–variance approach, MVO has perhaps not gained as much currency among practitioners as one might expect.

The main criticism of MVO in a practical setting is that implementing it from first principles requires investors to take views on a large number of parameters, particularly those relating to the expected returns of risk factors. Typically, investors have a small number of high-conviction views, which is not sufficient to run a full-blown optimization exercise. A related criticism is that mean–variance solutions can lead to large long–short positions in risk factors with high correlations, even if their Sharpe ratio differences were small and potentially caused by estimation error.

Several alternatives have been forwarded to address these concerns, the most notable being the "reverse optimization" method of Black and Litterman (1990). The Black–Litterman (BL) method takes a market portfolio as the starting point for the portfolio construction exercise. Further, it provides a convenient way, via Bayesian analysis, to blend an investor's small number of views with this starting point in order to arrive at an optimal portfolio. The BL setup is ideally suited for building portfolios of stocks in which the number of views that active investors might have tends to be quite small. However, the use of a "neutral point" as an exogenous input to the portfolio construction exercise is a convenient feature to incorporate into multi-asset contexts as well. Our discussion in this chapter has focused only on the determination of *active* tilts versus a neutral point, which could be a benchmark or a policy portfolio.

To deal with the issue of optimal solutions requiring large long–short positions, it is often useful to constrain relative value positions. In addition, it is essential to have an ongoing interaction between setting up the optimization problem and assessing the confidence in the inputs to it. For example, an investment process that emphasizes relative valuations of risk factors across countries or sectors should allocate a greater amount of the risk budget to relative value positions than one that is more top-down in nature.

The institutional context may necessitate modifications to the simplistic MVO approach. An asset manager who is mandated to manage portfolios against a fixed-income benchmark is typically expected to construct portfolios that outperform in regimes of economic weakness. Active overlays on such benchmarks ought to incorporate the additional constraint that they will not underperform significantly in weak economic conditions.

Despite these challenges, a formal portfolio construction exercise is an important tool to help portfolio managers navigate the complex trade-offs inherent in any large set of investment opportunities. With the judicious use of tail awareness, position constraints, and parsimony in problem formulation, even simple methodologies like MVO can yield rich insights into the optimal risk–return trade-off in realistic situations.

Appendix A.6.

A.6.1. Formal Specification of the Mean–Variance Optimization Program

The mean–variance optimization problem of a benchmarked investor is traditionally stated as follows. Let the benchmark and the portfolio consist of N securities (each with return $R(i)$, $i = 1, ..., N$), and denote by $\left[w^P(i) \right]_{i=1}^{N}$ and $\left[w^B(i) \right]_{i=1}^{N}$, respectively, the weights of various securities in the portfolio and the benchmark. Also denote the $N \times 1$ vector of expected returns on various securities by μ and their $N \times N$ covariance matrix by Σ_R. Then, the mean–variance problem of the investor is

$$\max_{\{w^P(i)\}_{i=1}^{N}} (\mu_P - \mu_B) \equiv \left[\sum_{i=1}^{N} [w^P(i) - w^B(i)] \mu(i) \right]$$

subject to the constraints

$$\left(w^P - w^B \right)^T \Sigma_R \left(w^P - w^B \right) \equiv \text{var}(R_P - R_B) \leq V^2,$$

$$\sum_{i=1}^{N} w^P(i) = \sum_{i=1}^{N} w^B(i) = 1,$$

Where w^P and w^B are the $N \times 1$ vectors of weights in the investor's portfolio and the benchmark and $[x]^T$ denotes the transpose of the vector x. It is clear from the formulation that the above portfolio selection problem is independent of the benchmark. We can simply think of the investor choosing the optimal over- and underweights $\left[w^P(i) - w^B(i) \right]$ to different assets in the benchmark.

As we have argued in the previous chapters, the difficulty in analyzing asset allocation via the above formulation is that the number of securities in a typical portfolio and benchmark could be quite large. For top-down construction of an optimal portfolio, we use risk factors to reduce dimensionality. It is this reformulation that we use in our optimal allocation exercise, as explained below.

The excess return on the benchmark (over the riskless rate) can be expressed in terms of its exposures to key risk factors

$$R_B(i) = \sum_{k=1}^{K} E_B(k)\tilde{f}(k) + \tilde{\delta}_B$$

where K is the small number of systematic risk factors used $(K \ll N)$, $\tilde{f}(k)$ is the realization of the kth factor (expressed as return on an appropriate zero-investment portfolio), $E_B(k)$ is the exposure of the benchmark to the kth risk factor, and $\tilde{\delta}_B$ is the part of the return of the benchmark that cannot be explained using the chosen risk factors. In a well-diversified benchmark and with a rich factor set, we expect the residual risk $\tilde{\delta}_B$ to be negligible. Now, we can formulate the asset allocation problem as a risk factor allocation problem. We choose a vector of exposures to the systematic risk factors that maximizes the expected excess return over the benchmark subject to a given limit on the variance of the excess return.

Letting the exposures in the chosen portfolio be $E_p(k)$, the excess return of the portfolio over the benchmark equals $\sum_{k=1}^{K} \tilde{E}_D(k)\tilde{f}(k) + \tilde{\delta}_B$ where $E_D(k) = E_P(k) - E_B(k)$ is the differential exposure of the portfolio (over the benchmark) to the kth risk factor. Thus, the mean–variance problem of the investor is given by

$$\max_{E_D \in \Re^K} [E_D]^T \mu_f$$

subject to the constraint

$$(E_D)^T \Sigma_f (E_D) \le V^2,$$

where μ_f is a $K \times 1$ vector of expected returns on the kth risk factor, Σ_f is a $K \times K$ covariance matrix of the risk factors, and $V \in \Re_{++}$ is the upper bound on portfolio volatility. We can also allow the investor to take exposure to risk factors that are off benchmark, to the extent that the investment mandate allows it.

In this simple setting, we obtain a closed-form analytical solution to the optimization program:

$$E_D^* = c\Sigma_f^{-1}\mu_f,$$ (6.1)

where E_D^* denotes the solution to the above optimization program and c is a scalar chosen so that the volatility of the portfolio equals V.[22] The key insight obtained from this solution is that the desirability of an investment ought to be assessed not by its standalone volatility but by its contribution to the volatility of the portfolio, which is a function of both the investment's own volatility and its covariation with other investments.

There is an alternative form of the optimal portfolio that is often useful. The covariance matrix Σ_f can be written in terms of the diagonal matrix of standard deviations of the returns on each risk factor, S, and the factor *correlation* matrix, ρ_p, as

$$\Sigma_f = S \times \rho_f \times S.$$

Then, Equation 6.1 is equivalent to

$$SE_D^* = c\rho_f^{-1}\lambda_f,$$

where $\lambda_f = S^{-1}\mu_f$ is the vector of *Sharpe ratios* of returns on various risk factors. Moreover, SE_D^* is the optimal exposure vector measured in terms of the standalone volatility generated by the exposure to each risk factor. Thus, if we define the exposures of a chosen portfolio to various risk factors in terms of their *standalone volatilities*, then the optimal solution depends only on the correlation matrix and the Sharpe ratios of various risk factors.

---

[22]The volatility constraint will bind as long as expected returns do not all equal zero and no additional constraints are imposed.

7. Moving beyond Stocks and Bonds: Alternative Investments

So far, we have concentrated on the problem of portfolio construction with traditional assets, such as equities, government bonds, and corporate bonds. In a real-life asset allocation exercise, the investor also has an opportunity to invest in a variety of so-called alternative investments. These investments can be classified broadly into three groups:

1. Private equity and venture capital

2. Real assets: real estate, infrastructure, farmland, timberland, and natural resources

3. Hedge funds and exotic beta strategies (momentum, carry, value, volatility, etc.)

In this chapter, we discuss the considerations that need to be accounted for when including alternatives in an optimal portfolio.

Alternative investments are an increasingly important component of the investment portfolios of longer-term investors, such as foundations, endowments, and sovereign wealth funds. According to the 2015 National Association of College and University Business Officers (NACUBO) study of US endowments, which covers 812 endowments that manage a total of $529 billion, 52% of the assets amongst participating institutions were classified as alternatives. This allocation compares to just 30% in 2004, highlighting a dramatic shift in asset allocation away from publicly traded equities and fixed income towards alternative investments in the last decade, following on another large shift in the same direction in the previous decade. At least part of this shift has been inspired by the much-publicized success and track record of the large US endowments, in particular those of Yale and Harvard.

Long-term investors generally expect to be able to earn a liquidity premium by investing in funds that require longer multiyear lockups, by directly or indirectly providing long-term financing to new enterprises in the economy (for instance, by being limited partners in a venture capital fund), and by investing in assets that are less liquid with higher transaction costs. Investors with more unpredictable liquidity needs and shorter investment horizons may shy away from such investments. In addition, alternatives are often viewed as effective diversifiers that exhibit fairly low correlation with equity risk and interest rates and have fairly low volatility and drawdowns. Their relatively high returns appear to come with low risk and significant diversification to other asset classes in normal times. Alternatives do appear to have been attractive historically, as shown in **Exhibit 7.1**.

In this chapter, we review the risk properties and diversification benefits of alternatives vis-à-vis publicly traded equities and bonds. We show that the lack of mark-to-market data may lure investors into the misconception that alternative asset classes and strategies represent something of a "free lunch." This misconception arises because return indices for privately held assets often are artificially smoothed, which biases both volatility and correlation estimates downward (particularly in down markets) and, correspondingly, biases measures of risk-adjusted performance, such as the Sharpe ratio, upward.

To address this problem, the statistical methods used to estimate correlations and volatilities must be adjusted to control for reporting biases in the illiquid return series. We show how to estimate risk factor exposures when the available asset return series may be smoothed due to the difficulty of obtaining market-based valuations. This adjustment provides a way of obtaining a more realistic view of the risks in alternative and illiquid investments. We find that alternative investments are exposed to many of the same risk factors as those that drive stock and bond returns. Risk models that fail to capture the systematic risk factor exposures of these investments may consequently overestimate their diversification benefits, resulting in the potential for over-investment in alternatives or higher-than-expected downside risk in crisis episodes.

The bottom line of our analysis in this chapter is that alternative investments are riskier than their reported index returns would generally suggest. Similarly, their correlations with other asset classes are higher once we control for reporting biases. These features of alternatives should be taken into account in selecting portfolios that can allocate risk to these assets.

Exhibit 7.1. **Excess Returns and Sharpe Ratios for Alternatives, December 1992–December 2015**

A. Excess Return

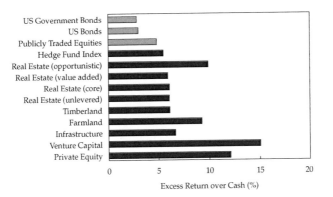

B. Sharpe Ratio

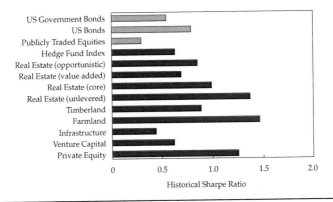

Notes: As of 31 December 2015. Data period is from December 1992 through December 2015. The models for Private Equity and Venture Capital are based on data from December 2001 to December 2015 and December 1996 to December 2015, respectively, whereas the infrastructure model is based on data since September 2000 due to data availability. The analysis is based on quarterly data, except for Timberland and Farmland where we use annual data frequency.

Sources: Bloomberg, Cambridge Associates, Kenneth French's website, National Council of Real Estate Investment Fiduciaries (NCREIF), PIMCO. Indices used for different asset classes and their underlying risk factors are as follows. *Private Equity*: Cambridge Associates US Private Equity Index. *Venture Capital*: Cambridge Associates US Venture Capital Index. *Infrastructure*: Macquarie Global Infrastructure Index. *Farmland*: NCREIF Farmland Property Index. *Timberland*: NCREIF Timberland Property Index. *Real Estate*: NCREIF Property Index, NCREIF Open-ended Core Diversified Equity Index, NCREIF-Townsend Value Added Funds Index, and NCREIF-Townsend Opportunistic Funds Index. *Hedge Funds*: Credit Suisse Hedge Fund Index. *U.S. Equity market, size and value factors*: Kenneth French Website. *U.S. Bonds*: Barclays US Aggregate Index. *US Government Bonds*: Barclays US Treasury index.

7.1. Risk Factor Exposures of Alternative Investments

The main challenge in including alternatives in an optimal portfolio with traditional assets is to model the exposure of alternatives to the same (or similar) risk factors to which traditional assets are exposed. An assessment of which factors to include requires the use of econometric methods as well as judgment. A "kitchen sink" regression approach, which starts from a large set of risk factors, however sophisticated it may be, will tend to isolate factors that improve the fit in sample but can produce exposures without a clear economic interpretation. For this reason, our approach to assigning risk factor exposures to alternative asset classes consists of two steps:

- First, we rely on economic intuition to narrow down the set of factors that should be relevant for a particular alternative asset class or strategy. This process relies on basic valuation principles and knowledge of the underlying investments.

- Second, we use econometric techniques to estimate exposures to each of the factors based on historical returns. To adjust for the smoothing effect, our model assumes that observed index returns represent a "moving average" of the current and past "true" investment returns. Dimson (1979) and Scholes and Williams (1977) present some of the theoretical foundations for this approach.[23]

As the first step in our empirical analysis, we discuss and identify the most important set of risk factors for each asset class.

If we accept that investors value alternative assets as discounted cash flow streams, we should expect their volatility to be driven mostly by the same factors that drive expected growth and discount rates for stocks and bonds. For assets with stable and less cyclical cash flow dynamics, valuation changes should be dominated by changes in interest rates—just as interest rates drive most of the volatility for bonds—while valuations for more speculative and highly cyclical investments should be driven by changes in the risk premia that investors require for risky assets and should consequently exhibit more equity-like characteristics.

Based on this logic, we posit that private equity, venture capital, and real assets are exposed to the following risk factors: the three Fama–French equity factors (i.e., equity market beta, small size, and value) and, additionally, credit spreads, real interest rates, and a liquidity factor.

---

[23]For other related but non-factor-based methods used to unsmooth data, see also Geltner (1993); Getmansky, Lo, and Makarov (2004); and Gallais-Hamonno and Nguyen-Thi-Thanh (2007).

Equity beta represents most of the mark-to-market risk across alternatives because equity market returns reflect changes in the way that investors value and discount risky cash flow streams at a broad level. As for corporate earnings, cash flows for private assets are linked to general economic growth. Company profitability and earnings growth can be expected to be high during expansions and low during recessions, irrespective of whether a specific company is traded privately or publicly. The same logic applies to real estate and infrastructure investments, whose cash flows—and therefore market values—vary with the level of economic activity. For example, a recession may reduce demand for office and retail space, which in turn negatively affects the occupancy rates and net operating income of commercial real estate properties. Hence, in general, changes in prospective equity market earnings should also be positively correlated with changes in projected cash flows from private investments.

Other equity factor betas help better capture asset class–specific risk exposures. Our models incorporate the size and value factors to account for exposures that may be independent of broad equity beta. Venture capital investments typically have strong growth (negative value) exposures, whereas other private equity strategies that aim at acquiring undervalued firms through levered buyouts can be characterized as having a distinct value tilt.

Credit spread duration captures bond-like cash flow risk and financing effects. While equity returns capture some of the common variation in discount rates across alternative asset classes, credit spreads may play a distinct role in shaping the returns for some alternatives, such as real estate and infrastructure. Due to the nature of their bond-like cash flows, the pricing of these real assets may fluctuate more directly with bond spreads than with equity valuations. In other words, credit spreads are a key component of the discount rate applied by investors to the cash flow streams of real asset investments because these assets are viewed in part as substitutes for bonds. In addition, most private equity, real estate, and infrastructure portfolios may be exposed to financing or refinancing risks. Due to this exposure, anticipated returns can be particularly vulnerable to changes in the cost and availability of debt financing, both of which change with credit spreads.

Real interest rate duration represents the inflation-hedging characteristics of certain alternative asset classes. Real estate investments, for instance, provide *real* cash flows that are broadly insensitive to the level of inflation and *nominal* cash flows that track inflation over the medium to long term. Rent payments can, for example, be modeled as cash flows that are similar to coupon payments on an inflation-indexed bond, since rent changes tend to reflect the general level of inflation. Similarly, managers of infrastructure

153

investments (such as toll roads and electricity producers) often have opportunities to at least partially adjust prices in response to inflation. Therefore, real estate and infrastructure investments could be particularly exposed to changes in real interest rates and less sensitive to changes in nominal rates. (In certain cases, where inflation pass-through is limited, it is appropriate to also consider assigning some nominal duration in the risk factor model.)

Liquidity beta represents an important, yet often overlooked, component of the investment risk of most alternative asset classes. Indeed, decisions to allocate to private and illiquid asset classes are often made without serious consideration of their exposure to liquidity risk. To capture the potential exposure of illiquid assets to fluctuations in liquidity, we include Pastor and Stambaugh's (2003) liquidity factor in our models for real estate, private equity, and infrastructure. The Pastor–Stambaugh factor captures excess returns on stocks that have large exposures to changes in aggregate liquidity. Pastor and Stambaugh construct their liquidity measure for each stock by estimating the return reversal effect associated with a given order flow (volume). They rely on the idea that lower-liquidity stocks will experience greater return reversals following high volume. These stock-level liquidity estimates are aggregated to form a marketwide liquidity measure at each point in time. The return to the liquidity risk factor in a given period is defined by the returns of a long–short portfolio of stocks that have been sorted according to their sensitivity to changes in market liquidity ("liquidity betas"). This methodology is similar to the methodology used to derive the Fama–French (1992) factors.

Recent academic research by Franzoni, Nowak, and Phalippou (2012) confirms that realized private equity returns are affected by their significant exposure to the Pastor–Stambaugh liquidity factor. The authors describe the economic channel that links private equity to public market liquidity, explaining how changes in illiquidity affect returns through the availability and costs of financing for private equity deals:

> Due to their high leverage, private equity investments are sensitive to the capital constraints faced by the providers of debt to private equity, who are primarily banks and hedge funds. Therefore, periods of low market liquidity are likely to coincide with periods when private equity managers may find it difficult to finance their investments, which in turn translate into lower returns for this asset class. (p. 2343)

The effects of funding liquidity and market liquidity are not confined to private real assets. Liquidity conditions should affect the viability of all levered investments and should drive correlation across assets, especially during stress periods. A common liquidity beta across alternative assets may help capture this effect.

It should be noted, however, that liquidity conditions generally fluctuate with aggregate market volatility and that changes in liquidity premia are also embedded in credit spreads; hence, the liquidity betas that we estimate must be interpreted as exposures to "incremental systemic liquidity," net of the liquidity effect embedded in other factors.

Risk Factors for Hedge Funds. One might consider a more extensive list of risk factors to capture the risks of hedge funds and include specialized "alternative beta"–type risk factors, such as FX carry, volatility, and momentum (trend following) in the analysis. We have found, however, that hedge fund style index returns are well explained by exposures to a conventional set of risk factors, and for that reason, we keep the set of risk factors parsimonious. The motivation for including hedge fund allocations in multi-asset portfolios is generally to diversify exposure to equity risk. It is therefore especially important to estimate the relationship between hedge fund returns and the equity factor and to evaluate how robust the relationship is likely to be in stressed markets. Most hedge fund styles tend to have significant exposures to equity risk (direct or indirect) that may lie dormant until a crisis occurs.

7.2. Econometric Estimation of Factor Exposures

We use an econometric model to estimate the factor exposures of alternatives. Our model accounts explicitly for the fact that the observed or reported returns on alternatives may suffer from a smoothing bias. We rely on the assumption that returns to a given asset can be expressed as a linear combination of risk factor returns. To derive the econometric specification, we assume that the observed "smoothed" returns for each of the illiquid assets can be viewed as a weighted average of the recent history of actual but unobserved returns. Thus, the observed return series on alternatives can be viewed as a so-called "moving average" process of past realized returns. If these realized (but unobserved) returns have a factor representation, then we can establish a relationship between *moving averages* of risk factor returns and the observed (smoothed) returns on alternatives. This relationship is then used to estimate jointly the factor betas and the moving average parameters that govern the degree of smoothing in observed returns. Details of the specification of the modes we use are given in the Appendix (item A.7.1).

Exhibit 7.2 shows the estimated risk factor exposures, using the method described above, for 11 indices of private equity, real asset, and hedge fund returns. The reported betas represent the estimated betas from the regression

Exhibit 7.2. Risk Factor Exposures and t-Statistics for Alternatives, December 1992–December 2015

Asset Class	US Equity	Size	Value	Liquidity (P&S)	Nominal Duration	Real Duration	Corporate Spread	Equity Beta (Univ.)
Private Equity	**0.5**	**-0.7**	**1.0**	**0.3**			**7.1**	**0.8**
	3.2	-1.6	1.8	1.1			2.6	8.2
Venture Capital	**1.1**	**-0.6**	**-5.0**					**1.6**
	5.2	-0.9	-8.4					6.1
Infrastructure	**0.7**					**3.3**	**4.5**	**0.7**
	5.9					2.2	2.0	8.9
Farmland	**0.2**					**10.4**		**0.1**
	1.0					1.5		0.3
Timberland	**0.4**					**11.3**		**0.1**
	2.8					3.2		1.11
Real Estate (Core)	**0.4**			**0.3**		**1.6**	**2.1**	**0.4**
	6.4			2.5		1.3	1.6	7.6
Real Estate (Core)	**0.5**			**0.4**		**2.5**	**3.5**	**0.5**
	6.5			2.6		1.6	2.0	7.8
Real Estate (Value Added)	**0.6**			**0.3**		**3.4**	**3.5**	**0.7**
	5.0			1.2		1.3	1.2	6.7
Real Estate (Opportunistic)	**0.6**			**0.1**		**3.0**	**13.8**	**0.9**
	3.8			0.4		0.8	3.6	6.2

(continued)

Exhibit 7.2. Risk Factor Exposures and t-Statistics for Alternatives, December 1992–December 2015 (continued)

Asset Class	US Equity	Size	Value	Liquidity (P&S)	Nominal Duration	Real Duration	Corporate Spread	Equity Beta (Univ.)
Hedge Funds	**0.4**	**0.2**					**1.7**	**0.4**
	5.4	1.2					1.2	8.7
Equities	**1.0**							**1.0**
	49.0							49.0
US Bonds					**4.7**		**2.3**	**0.0**
					16.8		7.3	-1.0
US Government Bonds					**5.4**			**0.2**
					28.6			-4.4

Notes: As of 31 December, 2015. Numbers in bold are coefficient from regressions estimated on adjusted risk factor returns based on the estimated lag structure in the index data (see Appendix for methodology), while numbers in italics are the Newey-West t-statistics. The return indices used for the asset classes are described in the footnote to Exhibit 7.1. Data period is generally from December 1992 through December 2015. The models for Private Equity and Venture Capital are based on data from December 2001 to December 2015, and December 1996 to December 2015 respectively, whereas the infrastructure model is based on data since September 2000 due to data availability. The analysis is based on quarterly data, except for Timberland and Farmland where we use annual data frequency.

Sources: Barclays, Bloomberg, Kenneth French's website, Lubos Pastor's website, PIMCO. Risk factor returns are from the following sources. *Equity market, size and value factors:* Kenneth French's Website. *Duration* (US 10 year Treasury yield): Bloomberg. *Real Duration* (US 10 year government yield minus 5 Year Inflation Expectations from OECD World Economic Outlook): Bloomberg. *Corporate credit spreads* (Barclays US Aggregate Credit Index option-adjusted spread): Bloomberg. *Liquidity factor* (Pastor-Stambaugh liquidity factor): Lubos Pastor's website (http://faculty.chicagobooth.edu/lubos.pastor/research/)

specification above. The exhibit also reports univariate regression equity betas, as well as risk exposures for equities and bonds, for comparison purposes.

7.3. Computing Risk Estimates

For all alternative investments discussed in this chapter, **Exhibit 7.3** compares volatilities based on published index returns with estimated (unsmoothed) index return volatilities from our model. Estimated volatility can be decomposed into two components:

- *Factor-based volatility.* To estimate volatility from risk factors for a given asset class, we use the standard portfolio risk formula, but we replace weights, volatilities, and correlations with risk factor exposures, risk factor volatilities, and risk factor correlations.

- *Non-factor-based volatility (idiosyncratic risk).* We add idiosyncratic volatility such that total volatility matches the unsmoothed index volatility. Idiosyncratic volatility can come from security selection, factor timing, and a variety of other nonsystematic, non-factor-based risk exposures. Idiosyncratic volatility is assumed to have zero correlation with factor-based volatility.

The values reported in Exhibit 7.3 show the contributions from systematic (factor) and idiosyncratic volatilities to the total adjusted volatility. This analysis reveals, as expected, that volatilities calculated directly from index returns are much lower than those from our unsmoothed estimates. Unsmoothing the returns data increases volatility across *all* asset classes. For certain asset classes, the difference is material. In general, private equity and real estate exhibit more evidence of a smoothing bias than do hedge funds. Risk estimates for venture capital, real estate, and private equity therefore appear particularly sensitive to the correction.

The exhibit also shows the results for an *F*-test used to measure whether the differences between reported and adjusted volatilities are statistically significant (i.e., before versus after adjusting for serial correlation). A result of 0% indicates a near certainty that the volatilities are different. Only listed infrastructure, equities, and US treasuries fail this test, which is expected, as these are public market indices. A few of the risk factors themselves are serially correlated due to valuation and liquidity effects. In particular, *F*-tests suggest significant smoothing for credit spread and value factors.

Exhibit 7.4 shows the difference between adjusted return volatilities and reported volatilities (from index returns) for several alternative investments, as well as for public markets (equities and bonds). This exhibit highlights

Exhibit 7.3. Volatilities, Correlations, and Equity Betas: Reported vs. Adjusted, December 1992–December 2015

	Volatilities					Equity Correlations		Equity Betas	
	Reported	Adjusted	Factors	Idiosync.	F-Test	Reported	Adjusted	Reported	Adjusted
Private Equity	10%	20%	15%	6%	0%	77%	67%	0.4	0.8
Venture Capital	24%	50%	34%	16%	0%	45%	42%	0.6	1.3
Infrastructure (Listed)	15%	17%	13%	4%	42%	76%	75%	0.6	0.7
Farmland	6%	15%	9%	6%	0%	2%	-18%	0.0	-0.1
Timberland	7%	13%	9%	4%	2%	8%	-1%	0.0	0.0
Real Estate (Unlevered)	4%	12%	7%	5%	0%	16%	54%	0.0	0.4
Real Estate (Core)	6%	17%	10%	7%	0%	13%	55%	0.0	0.6
Real Estate (Value Added)	9%	21%	12%	10%	0%	16%	51%	0.1	0.6
Real Estate (Opportunistic)	12%	31%	17%	14%	0%	30%	49%	0.2	0.9
Hedge Fund Index	9%	11%	8%	3%	6%	74%	71%	0.4	0.4
Equities	17%	18%	18%	0%	44%	99%	98%	1.0	1.0
US Bonds	4%	5%	4%	1%	2%	-14%	-17%	0.0	0.0
US Treasuries	5%	6%	6%	0%	26%	-52%	-52%	-0.1	-0.2

Notes: As of 31 December, 2015. See notes to Exhibits 7.1 and 7.2 for further details about sources for returns for asset classes and risk factors.

Exhibit 7.4.   Difference between Reported and Adjusted Volatility and Autocorrelation Measure by Asset Class, December 1992–December 2015

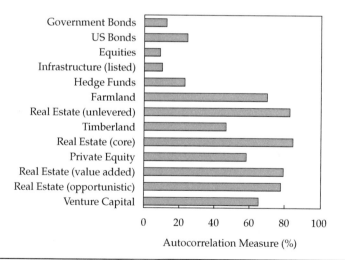

A. Volatility

B. Autocorrelation

Notes: As of 31 December 2015. See notes to Exhibits 7.1 and 7.2 for further details about sources for returns for asset classes and risk factors.

just how much return smoothing results in underestimation of volatility and risk. The bias tends to be more pronounced for indices that are more heavily smoothed, as captured by the autocorrelation of reported returns. The autocorrelation measure that is shown below the volatility adjustments is the sum of the coefficients on significant lags using the methodology outlined in this section (i.e., it is the weight of past returns in the current index return). The number of significant lags ("Q" from Equation 2 in the Appendix to this chapter) is two years for timberland and farmland, five quarters for venture capital and private equity, six quarters for all real estate asset classes, and one quarter for listed infrastructure, stocks, and bonds.

The historical risk-adjusted returns of all alternative investments are reduced in proportion to the increase in measured volatility. The average historical Sharpe ratio of the alternative investments in infrastructure, hedge funds, real estate, private equity, farmland, and timberland is almost cut in half (from 0.81 to 0.44) after the volatilities have been adjusted to a more appropriate level. Again, the alternative assets with the most smoothed return series, such as real estate, are affected the most by our adjustments of risk, whereas the adjustments to hedge fund returns are relatively minor. The Sharpe ratio of public equities is 0.36 over the same time period. It follows that the relative attractiveness of alternatives in terms of their risk-adjusted returns indeed is quite sensitive to the measurement of their risk.

In **Exhibit 7.5**, we also compare correlations to equities and equity betas for published returns with estimates based on our models. Because we use common risk factors with equities—including direct equity beta—it is not surprising to see that our models generate higher (and, we argue, more realistic) equity correlations and equity betas. The differences are large in some cases, and equity betas are higher across the board, reflecting both the higher revised correlations and the higher volatilities.

161

Exhibit 7.5a. **Difference between Reported and Adjusted Historical Sharpe Ratios, Equity Correlations, and Equity Betas by Asset Class, December 1992–December 2015**

A. Sharpe Ratio

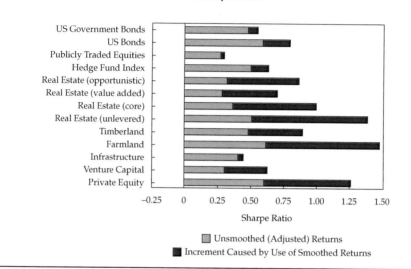

Exhibit 7.5b. **Difference between Reported and Adjusted Historical Sharpe Ratios, Equity Correlations, and Equity Betas by Asset Class, December 1992–December 2015**

B. Estimated Equity Correlation

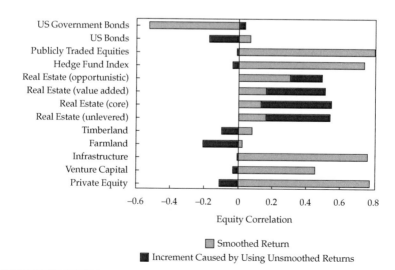

Exhibit 7.5c. **Difference between Reported and Adjusted Historical Sharpe Ratios, Equity Correlations, and Equity Betas by Asset Class, December 1992– December 2015**

C. Estimated Beta to Publicly Traded Equities

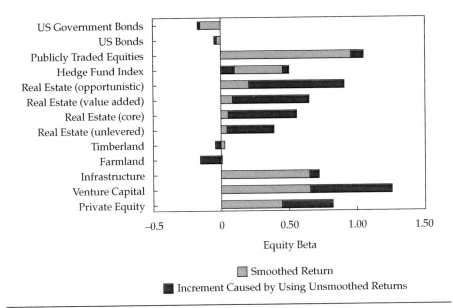

Notes: As of 31 December 2015. See notes to Exhibits 7.1 and 7.2 for further details about sources for returns for asset classes and risk factors. Panel A: The sums of the two bars represent Sharpe ratios using the volatility of index (smoothed) returns. Panel B: The sums of the two bars represent correlations of the unsmoothed (adjusted) returns. Panel C: The sums of the two represent betas of the unsmoothed (adjusted) returns.

Exhibit 7.6 illustrates how our adjustments to the risks and correlations of alternatives affects estimates of portfolio risk. In this exhibit, we present portfolios of an increasing number of asset classes, starting from the most liquid (stocks and bonds) and incrementally adding the following key illiquid assets: private equity, real estate, farmland, and timberland. All portfolios are equally weighted ("1/n" portfolios). As the number of assets increases, risk goes down, and the curvature of the plot tells us about the effect of diversification.

Starting from the left, volatility estimates for stocks and bonds are quite similar. The effect of unsmoothing index data for liquid markets is unlikely to be statistically significant. Next, private equity adds risk to a portfolio of stocks and bonds. We expect this result because private equity's volatility is more than twice as high as that of an equally weighted portfolio of stocks and bonds. Crucially, as we add illiquid assets, the two lines start to diverge. Our

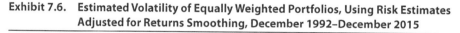

Exhibit 7.6. Estimated Volatility of Equally Weighted Portfolios, Using Risk Estimates Adjusted for Returns Smoothing, December 1992–December 2015

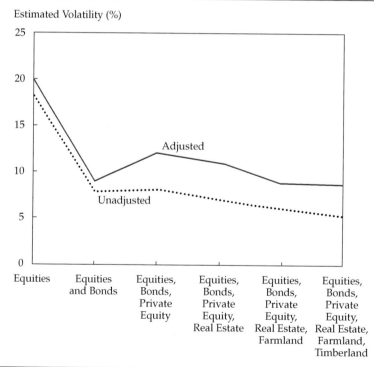

Notes: As of 31 December 2015. See notes to Exhibit 7.1 and 7.2 for further details about sources for returns for asset classes and risk factors.

estimate of unsmoothed portfolio volatility for the six-asset portfolio remains relatively high at 8.8%, compared to 5.3% for the estimate based on reported index returns. This significant difference is due to our volatility adjustments and also to the increase in implied correlations amongst all assets in the portfolio (due to the use of common mark-to-market risk factors). A volatility of 8.8% is not too far from the volatility of the initial portfolio of stocks and bonds (9.0%).

Caveats on Hedge Fund Models. For hedge fund risk analysis and manager selection, it is particularly important to complement the risk factor approach with other approaches. Risk factor analysis cannot replace the due diligence process that provides a more holistic view of individual managers' activities.

Also, it may be ill advised to map an individual hedge fund to risk factors based on its hedge fund style category's exposures, because individual hedge funds often deviate substantially from their peers or from the average fund in their category. Some of the managers may also be selling or buying options, giving rise to nonlinear factor exposures that become evident only in tail events and crisis episodes. These exposures can be difficult to identify during periods when financial markets are well behaved. Access to short-term funding is important to most hedge funds, since they rely on significant leverage to achieve their investment objectives or to implement relative value strategies. Note that we do not explicitly address the risk associated with "forced" deleveraging in episodes of financial crisis in our risk factor models, but this is an important dimension of the tail risk for hedge funds. We also note that there is potential for direct or indirect contagion across hedge funds due to the complex and illiquid nature of the fund activities. These joint dependencies are naturally extremely challenging to model and are beyond the scope of our risk factor analysis.

7.4. The Bottom Line on Risk Factor Models for Alternatives

Mean–variance optimization based on smoothed return indices typically suggests extremely high optimal allocations to alternative assets, due to their low realized volatility and low correlation vis-à-vis publicly traded investments in liquid markets. However, in many cases, public and private investment vehicles provide exposure to the same underlying assets and represent claims to similar or highly correlated cash flows. Consequently, public and private investments in the same underlying asset or economic activity should be distinct only from the point of view of liquidity, tax structure, dividend distribution profile, and to some extent, leverage. Any risk model that assigns very different levels of risk and factor exposures to two otherwise very similar investments would seem to be fundamentally flawed.

Our risk factor framework and our econometric modeling approach reveal that alternative assets indeed have significant exposure to the same risk factors that drive volatility in publicly traded stocks and bonds. Returns on alternative assets depend on changes in interest rates, as well as the way that investors value risky cash flows, as reflected in equity market valuations and credit spreads. Lastly, liquidity and other specialized factors also play a role. In addition to higher volatility, expected drawdowns, and tail risk exposures, the risk factor–based approach generally generates higher correlations between alternative investments and their public market counterparts, especially when their equity beta is high.

Nonetheless, our approach should *not necessarily* lead investors to avoid illiquid assets. This approach simply means investors should require a higher rate of return than they would otherwise. Long-term investors may still be able to consistently (in equilibrium) earn a liquidity premium by committing long-term financing and capital (debt or equity) to various privately held enterprises or through investments in funds that can acquire and keep assets that cannot be easily liquidated, if at all. Also, the characteristics of privately held assets can appeal to different investors and segments of the market and thereby possibly drive a wedge between the valuations in private and public markets, and the expected returns of privately held assets may differ at different phases of the business cycle and/or funding cycle.

Overall, we recognize that our risk factor models can only go so far in describing the risks of alternative assets, but our approach should perform better (in the sense of giving a more accurate picture of potential drawdowns and volatility) than simply using artificially smoothed index returns. Importantly, our modeling approach provides a coherent framework for aggregating risk exposures across public markets and alternative investments.

Appendix A.7.

A.7.1. Econometric Estimation of the Factor Exposures of Alternative Investments

To estimate the factor betas of returns on alternative investments when we can observe only a "smoothed" series of returns, we first postulate that the true (but unobserved) returns are given by

$$r_t = \alpha + \sum_i \beta_i f_{i,t} + \varepsilon_t, \tag{7.1}$$

where r_t is the return of the asset, α is the intercept, β_i is the exposure of the asset to the ith factor, $f_{i,t}$ is the return on the ith factor, and ε_t is an error term.

Then, we assume that the observed "smoothed" returns for each of the illiquid assets can be viewed as a weighted average of the recent history of the above actual but unobserved returns, as shown in Equation (7.2):

$$r_{obs,t} = \sum_{j}^{Q} \omega_j r_{t-j},\qquad(7.2)$$

where $r_{obs,t}$ is the observed index return, Q is the number of lags, r_t is the unobserved actual investment return, and $\{\omega_j\}$ are weights that reflect how past realized investment returns affect the current observed, smoothed return. The weights are assumed/normalized to satisfy the conditions $\sum_{j}^{Q}\omega_j = 1$, $\omega_j > 0$. The observed return series, r_{obs}, can thus be viewed as a so-called "moving average" process of past investment returns, r, with normalized coefficients equal to $\{\omega_j\}$.[24]

The observed index return can now be written as a function of past risk factor returns, as shown in Equation 7.3:

$$r_{obs,t} = \sum_{j}^{Q}\omega_j\left(\alpha + \sum_{i}^{N}\beta_i f_{i,t-j} + \varepsilon_{t-j}\right) = \sum_{j}^{Q}\omega_j\alpha + \sum_{i}^{N}\beta_i\sum_{j}^{Q}\omega_j f_{i,t-j} + \sum_{j}^{Q}\omega_j\varepsilon_{t-j},\qquad(7.3)$$

where N is the number of risk factors. If we define $X_{i,t} = \sum_{j}^{Q}\omega_j f_{i,t-j}$ as the transformed (moving average) risk factor returns and $\eta_t = \sum_{j}^{Q}\omega_j\varepsilon_{t-j}$ as the weighted error term, it then follows that we can estimate risk factor betas (β_j) on $X_{i,t}$ directly, as shown in Equation (7.4):

$$r_{obs,t} = \alpha + \sum_{i}^{N}\beta_i X_{i,t} + \eta_t.\qquad(7.4)$$

The parameters of this joint model of actual and smoothed illiquid asset returns can be estimated in two steps. The lag weights (ω_j) are first estimated with maximum likelihood on observed (smoothed) asset returns.

---

[24]The specification implies an MA(q) process for returns. This approach is based on the additional assumption that actual returns are identically and independently distributed over time. The parameters of the MA(q) process can be estimated using standard software packages. We use the ARMAX filter function in MATLAB (from Kevin Sheppard's Econometrics Toolbox, available at www.kevinsheppard.com). The estimation process also gives us an estimate of the actual unsmoothed investment returns.

For each asset, an appropriate number of lags are selected based on their statistical significance. In the second step, these estimates for (ω_j) are used to construct the appropriately weighted factor return time series ($X_{i,t}$). The factor loadings $\{\beta_j\}$ are then estimated from Equation 7.4 using ordinary least squares. Since the error terms, η_t, will be autocorrelated, we use Newey–West corrected standard errors to assess statistical significance for each of the estimated factor exposures.

Bibliography

Back, K. 2010. *Asset Pricing and Portfolio Choice Theory*. New York: Oxford University Press.

Ben Dor, A., and Z. Xu. 2011. "Fallen Angels: Characteristics, Performance, and Implications for Investors." *Journal of Fixed Income*, vol. 20, no. 4 (Spring): 33–58.

Ben Dor, A., L. Dynkin, J. Hyman, P. Houweling, E. van Leeuwen, and O. Penninga. 2007. "DTS (Duration Times Spread)." *Journal of Portfolio Management*, vol. 33, no. 2 (Winter): 77–100.

Black, F., and R. Litterman. 1990. "Asset Allocation: Combining Investor Views with Market Equilibrium." Goldman Sachs Fixed Income Research (September).

Campbell, J., and R. Shiller. 1988. "Stock Prices, Earnings, and Expected Dividends." *Journal of Finance*, vol. 43, no. 3 (July): 661–676.

Campbell, J., A. Lo, and C. McKinley. 1996. *The Econometrics of Financial Markets*. Princeton: Princeton University Press.

Campbell, J., A. Sunderam, and L. Viceira. 2013. "Inflation Bets or Deflation Hedges? The Changing Risks of Nominal Bonds." Working Paper 09-088, Harvard Business School.

Carr, P., and V. Linetsky. 2006. "A Jump to Default Extended CEV Model: An Application of Bessel Processes." *Finance and Stochastics*, vol. 10, no. 3 (September): 303–330.

Cochrane, J. 2005. *Asset Pricing*, rev. ed. Princeton: Princeton University Press.

———. 2008. "The Dog That Did Not Bark: A Defense of Return Predictability." *Review of Financial Studies*, vol. 21, no. 4: 1533–1575.

———. 2014. "A Mean-Variance Benchmark for Intertemporal Portfolio Theory." *Journal of Finance*, vol. 69, no. 1 (February): 1–49.

Cochrane, J., and C. Culp. 2003. "Equilibrium Asset Pricing and Discount Factors: Overview and Implications for Derivatives Valuation and Risk Management." In *Modern Risk Management: A History*. Edited by Peter Field. London: Risk Books.

Davydov, D., and V. Linetsky. 2001. "Pricing and Hedging Path-Dependent Options under the CEV Process." *Management Science*, vol. 47, no. 7 (July): 949–965.

Dimson, E. 1979. "Risk Measurement When Shares Are Subject to Infrequent Trading." *Journal of Financial Economics*, vol. 7, no. 2 (June): 197–226.

Dimson, E., P. Marsh, and M. Staunton. 2013a. *Credit Suisse Global Investment Returns Sourcebook 2013*. Zurich: Credit Suisse Research Institute.

———. 2013b. *Dimson-Marsh-Staunton (DMS) Global Investment Returns Database*. New York: Morningstar.

Duffie, D. 2002. *Dynamic Asset Pricing Theory*. Princeton: Princeton University Press.

Engle, R. 1982. "Autoregressive Conditional Heteroskedasticity with Estimates of the Variance of UK Inflation." *Econometrica*, vol. 50, no. 4 (July): 987–1008.

Fama, E., and R. Bliss. 1987. "The Information in Long-Maturity Forward Rates." *Journal of Financial Economics*, vol. 77, no. 4 (September): 680–692.

Fama, E., and K. French. 1992. "The Cross-Section of Expected Stock Returns." *Journal of Finance*, vol. 47, no. 2 (June): 427–464.

Franzoni, F., E. Nowak, and L. Phalippou. 2012. "Private Equity Performance and Liquidity Risk." *Journal of Finance*, vol. 67, no. 6 (December): 2341–2373.

Frazzini, A., and L. Pedersen. 2014. "Betting against Beta." *Journal of Financial Economics*, vol. 111, no. 1 (January): 1–25.

Gallais-Hamonno, G., and H. Nguyen-Thi-Thanh. 2007. "The Necessity to Correct Hedge Fund Returns: Empirical Evidence and Correction Method." Working Paper CEB 07-034.RS, Université Libre de Bruxelles.

Geltner, D. 1993. "Estimating Market Values from Appraised Values without Assuming an Efficient Market." *Journal of Real Estate Research*, vol. 8, no. 3 (Summer): 325–346.

Getmansky, M., A. Lo, and I. Makarov. 2004. "An Econometric Model of Serial Correlation and Illiquidity in Hedge Fund Returns." *Journal of Financial Economics*, vol. 74, no. 3 (July): 529–609.

Gordon, M., and E. Shapiro. 1956. "Capital Equipment Analysis: The Required Rate of Profit." *Management Science*, vol. 3, no. 1 (October): 102–110.

Gurkaynak, R., D. Sack, and J. Wright. 2006. "The U.S. Treasury Yield Curve: 1961 to the Present." Finance and Economics Discussion Series No. 2006-28 (June): http://www.federalreserve.gov/pubs/feds/2006/200628/200628abs.html.

Hansen, L., and R. Jagannathan. 1991. "Restrictions on Intertemporal Marginal Rates of Substitution Implied by Asset Returns." *Journal of Political Economy*, vol. 99: 225–262.

Heston, S., and K.G. Rouwenhorst. 1995. "Industry and Country Effects in International Stock Returns: Implications for Asset Allocation." *Journal of Portfolio Management*, vol. 21, no. 3 (Spring): 53–58.

Ilmanen, A. 2011. *Expected Returns: An Investor's Guide to Harvesting Market Rewards*. Hoboken, NJ: John Wiley & Sons.

Jegadeesh, N., and S. Titman. 1993. "Returns from Buying Winners and Selling Losers: Implications for Stock Market Efficiency." *Journal of Finance*, vol. 48, no. 1 (March): 65–91.

Leibowitz, M., W. Krasker, and A. Nozari. 1990. "Spread Duration: A New Tool for Bond Portfolio Management." *Journal of Portfolio Management*, vol. 16, no. 3 (Spring): 46–53.

Litterman, R., and J. Scheinkman. 1991. "Common Factors Affecting Bond Returns." *Journal of Fixed Income*, vol. 1, no. 1 (June): 54–61.

Markowitz, H. 1952. "Portfolio Selection." *Journal of Finance*, vol. 7, no. 1 (March): 77–91.

Mehra, R. 2008. "The Equity Premium Puzzle: A Review." *Foundations and Trends in Finance*, vol. 2, no. 1: 1–81.

Mehra, R., and E. Prescott. 1985. "The Equity Premium: A Puzzle." *Journal of Monetary Economics*, vol. 15, no. 2 (March): 145–161.

Merton, R. 1974. "On the Pricing of Corporate Debt: The Risk Structure of Interest Rates." *Journal of Finance*, vol. 29, no. 2 (May): 449–470.

———. 1980. "On Estimating the Expected Returns on the Market: An Exploratory Investigation." *Journal of Financial Economics*, vol. 8, no. 4 (December): 323–361.

———. 1992. *Continuous-Time Finance*. Walden, MA: Blackwell Publishing.

————. 2011. "The Equity Premium Puzzle Revisited." In *Rethinking the Equity Risk Premium*. Edited by P. Brett Hammond, Martin L. Leibowitz, and Laurence B. Siegel. Charlottesville, VA: CFA Institute Research Foundation.

Moore, J. 2013. "Who's Buying Now? Some Long-Term Investors Are Snapping Up Bonds." *Institutional Investor*, vol. 8, July.

Ng, Kwok-Yuen, and B. Phelps. 2011. "Capturing Credit Spread Premium." *Financial Analysts Journal*, vol. 67, no. 3 (May/June): 63–75.

Pastor, L., and R. Stambaugh. 2003. "Liquidity Risk and Expected Stock Returns." *Journal of Political Economy*, vol. 111, no. 3 (June): 642–685.

Rubinstein, M. 1976. "The Valuation of Uncertain Income Streams and the Pricing of Options." *Bell Journal of Economics*, vol. 7, no. 2 (Autumn): 407–425.

————. 2006. *A History of the Theory of Investments*. Hoboken, NJ: John Wiley & Sons.

Scholes, M., and J. Williams. 1977. "Estimating Betas from Nonsynchronous Data." *Journal of Financial Economics*, vol. 5, no. 3 (December): 309–327.

Shiller, R. 1981. "Do Stock Prices Move Too Much to Be Justified by Subsequent Changes in Dividends?" *American Economic Review*, vol. 71, no. 3 (June): 421–436.

Surz, Ronald J. 2016. "The 90-Year History of Capital Market Returns and Risks." Nasdaq (15 February): http://www.nasdaq.com/article/the-90-year-history-of-capital-market-returns-and-risks-cm579889.

Verdelhan, A. 2015. "Share of Systematic Variation in Bilateral Exchange Rates." SSRN: http://dx.doi.org/10.2139/ssrn.1930516.

Wilcox, S. 2007. "The Adjusted Earnings Yield." *Financial Analysts Journal*, vol. 63, no. 5: 54–68.

Zhang, L. 2005. "The Value Premium." *Journal of Finance*, vol. 60, no. 1 (February): 67–103.

Named Endowments

The CFA Institute Research Foundation acknowledges with sincere gratitude the generous contributions of the Named Endowment participants listed below.

Gifts of at least US$100,000 qualify donors for membership in the Named Endowment category, which recognizes in perpetuity the commitment toward unbiased, practitioner-oriented, relevant research that these firms and individuals have expressed through their generous support of the CFA Institute Research Foundation.

Ameritech
Anonymous
Robert D. Arnott
Theodore R. Aronson, CFA
Asahi Mutual Life
Batterymarch Financial
  Management
Boston Company
Boston Partners Asset Management,
  L.P.
Gary P. Brinson, CFA
Brinson Partners, Inc.
Capital Group International, Inc.
Concord Capital Management
Dai-Ichi Life Company
Daiwa Securities
Mr. and Mrs. Jeffrey Diermeier
Gifford Fong Associates
Investment Counsel Association
  of America, Inc.
Jacobs Levy Equity Management
John A. Gunn, CFA
John B. Neff, CFA
Jon L. Hagler Foundation
Long-Term Credit Bank of Japan, Ltd.
Lynch, Jones & Ryan, LLC
Meiji Mutual Life Insurance
  Company

Miller Anderson & Sherrerd, LLP
Nikko Securities Co., Ltd.
Nippon Life Insurance Company of
  Japan
Nomura Securities Co., Ltd.
Payden & Rygel
Provident National Bank
Frank K. Reilly, CFA
Salomon Brothers
Sassoon Holdings Pte. Ltd.
Scudder Stevens & Clark
Security Analysts Association
  of Japan
Shaw Data Securities, Inc.
Sit Investment Associates, Inc.
Standish, Ayer & Wood, Inc.
State Farm Insurance Company
Sumitomo Life America, Inc.
T. Rowe Price Associates, Inc.
Templeton Investment Counsel Inc.
Frank Trainer, CFA
Travelers Insurance Co.
USF&G Companies
Yamaichi Securities Co., Ltd.

Senior Research Fellows

Financial Services Analyst Association

For more on upcoming Research Foundation
publications and webcasts, please visit
www.cfainstitute.org/learning/foundation.

Research Foundation monographs
are online at www.cfapubs.org.

RESEARCH FOUNDATION
CONTRIBUTION FORM

☑ **Yes**, I want the Research Foundation to continue to fund innovative research that advances the investment management profession. Please accept my tax-deductible contribution at the following level:

Thought Leadership Circle.................... US$1,000,000 or more
Named Endowment...................... US$100,000 to US$999,999
Research Fellow .... US$10,000 to US$99,999
Contributing Donor........................... US$1,000 to US$9,999
Friend .... Up to US$999

I would like to donate US$ _____.

☐ My check is enclosed (payable to the CFA Institute Research Foundation).
☐ I would like to donate appreciated securities (send me information).
☐ Please charge my donation to my credit card.
　　　　☐ VISA ☐ MC ☐ Amex ☐ Diners

|||||||||||||||||||

Card Number

_____ / _____
Expiration Date　　　　　　　　Name on card　PLEASE PRINT

☐ Corporate Card
☐ Personal Card

　　　　　　　　　　　　　　Signature

☐ This is a pledge. Please bill me for my donation of US$_____
☐ I would like recognition of my donation to be:
　　☐ Individual donation ☐ Corporate donation ☐ Different individual

_____
PLEASE PRINT NAME OR COMPANY NAME AS YOU WOULD LIKE IT TO APPEAR

PLEASE PRINT ☐ Mr. ☐ Mrs. ☐ Ms.　MEMBER NUMBER_____

Last Name (Family Name)　　　First (Given Name)　　　Middle Initial

Title

Address

City　　　　　　　State/Province　　Country ZIP/Postal Code

Please mail this completed form with your contribution to:
The CFA Institute Research Foundation • P.O. Box 2082
Charlottesville, VA 22902-2082 USA

For more on the CFA Institute Research Foundation, please visit www.cfainstitute.org/learning/foundation/Pages/index.aspx.

88436462R00106

Made in the USA
San Bernardino, CA
12 September 2018